ANDREW JOHNSON

PRESIDENTIAL ✦ LEADERS

ANDREW JOHNSON

KATE HAVELIN

⌐ LERNER PUBLICATIONS COMPANY/MINNEAPOLIS

This book is for my son, Max Timmons, who loves history—
especially history far older than this.

Lerner Publications Company
A division of Lerner Publishing Group
241 First Avenue North
Minneapolis, MN 55401 U.S.A.

Website address: www.lernerbooks.com

Library of Congress Cataloging-in-Publication Data

Havelin, Kate, 1961–
    Andrew Johnson / Kate Havelin.
      p.   cm. — (Presidential leaders)
    Summary: Follows the life and career of the statesman who became the seventeenth president of the United States after the assassination of Abraham Lincoln.
    Includes bibliographical references and index.
    ISBN: 0–8225–1000–6 (lib. bdg. : alk. paper)
    1. Johnson, Andrew, 1808–1875—Juvenile literature. 2. Presidents—United States— Biography—Juvenile literature. [1. Johnson, Andrew, 1808-1875. 2. Presidents.] I. Title. II. Series.
E667.H385   2005
973.8'1'092—dc22   2003022351

Manufactured in the United States of America
1 2 3 4 5 6 – JR – 10 09 08 07 06 05

CONTENTS

———— ✧ ————

INTRODUCTION 7

1 **ROUGH START** 10

2 **AMBITIOUS TAILOR TO
MECHANIC GOVERNOR** 19

3 **WAR** 31

4 **VICE PRESIDENT, THEN PRESIDENT** 43

5 **PRESIDENTIAL RECONSTRUCTION** 54

6 **A "DEAD DOG" PRESIDENT** 66

7 **IMPEACHED!** 81

8 **LIFE AFTER IMPEACHMENT** 95

TIMELINE 104

SOURCE NOTES 106

BIBLIOGRAPHY 108

FURTHER READING AND WEBSITES 109

INDEX 110

*President Andrew Johnson first went to Washington, D.C.,
as a U.S. senator from Tennessee.*

INTRODUCTION

My efforts have been to preserve the Union of these States. I never, for a single moment, entertained the opinion that a State could withdraw from the Union of its own will.

—Andrew Johnson

When the Civil War between the North and the South started in 1861, Andrew Johnson was one of the most hated people in the South. He was a Southerner who sided with the North, believing that the U.S. Constitution didn't allow states to secede, or leave, the Union.

Johnson was a U.S. senator when South Carolina became the first Southern state to secede from the Union in December 1860. Within months several more states also seceded. They joined to form the Confederate States of America, or the Confederacy, and war broke out between the Confederacy and the Union.

Johnson, a Southerner by birth, showed his faith in the Union by continuing to serve in the U.S. Congress. He was the only Southern member of Congress to stay in

Washington, D.C., during the war. Worried that his home state of Tennessee would also secede, Johnson took the train home in February 1861 to see his family and to try to convince his fellow Tennesseans to stay in the Union.

On the journey home, Johnson's courage and his beliefs were tested. Riding the train south from Washington, Johnson faced mobs that wanted to hurt him. When the train stopped in Liberty, Virginia, a crowd of angry Southerners stormed the train and rushed Johnson. When they threatened him, the senator pulled out his pistol and held the mob at bay until they went away. As the train left town, the defiant Johnson yelled a fiery message to the crowd: "I am a Union man!"

Crowds in Lynchburg, Virginia, were more violent. They dragged Johnson from the train, spit on him, kicked him, and threatened to hang him. They tied a rope around his neck and dragged Johnson to a tree. Soon the senator who was staying loyal to the Union would be lynched by fellow Southerners.

Johnson's life was saved by an old man, who shouted to the crowd that they didn't have the right to kill the senator. "His neighbors in Greeneville [Tennessee] have made arrangements to hang their Senator on his arrival," the old man yelled. "Virginians have no right to deprive them of that privilege."

Those insulting words saved Johnson's life. But it took the actions of another Southerner to protect the outspoken senator. Confederate president Jefferson Davis decided that Johnson would do the South less harm alive then dead. Davis feared that if Johnson were killed, his death would spark outrage in the North and would inspire Northerners to hold firm and attack the South. Davis ordered that the train carrying Johnson keep moving along regardless of mobs. So Davis, the leader of Southern states that had seceded from the Union, saved the life of Andrew Johnson, a Southern senator who didn't believe states had the right to secede.

Johnson went home to Tennessee and continued to speak out forcefully against secession and against the war. His strong stand made him countless enemies in the South, where people called him a traitor. But Johnson's impassioned views earned him just as many supporters in the North, where he was seen as a patriot. The *New York Times* wrote, "His name is in every mouth today, and he is freely applauded as the greatest man of the age."

Patriot or traitor, Johnson stood up for what he believed in. Along with the death threats, his defense of the Union earned him praise and power. In 1862 President Lincoln appointed Johnson the military governor of Tennessee. In 1864 Johnson was Lincoln's running mate, and, when Lincoln was assassinated in April 1865, Andrew Johnson became the seventeenth president of the United States.

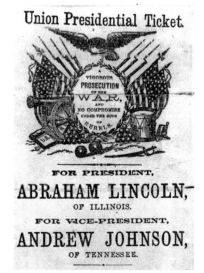

——————————— ✧

The 1864 Lincoln-Johnson presidential ballot promises "a vigorous prosecution of the war, and no compromise under the guns of rebels [Confederates]."

CHAPTER ONE

ROUGH START

*I have grappled with the gaunt and haggard
monster called hunger.*

—Andrew Johnson

On the chilly night of December 29, 1808, in Raleigh, North Carolina, Casso's Inn was full of people. They were celebrating the wedding of the tavern owner's daughter. Behind the inn, in a tiny wooden cabin with a dirt floor, Mary Johnson gave birth to a son to be named Andrew.

Jacob Johnson and his wife, Mary McDonough Johnson, were two of Raleigh's one thousand residents. Mary sewed and did laundry for Raleigh's wealthier families. Jacob did odd jobs around town. The couple had three children—William, Elizabeth, and Andrew.

Andrew was one of eight presidents born in log cabins, but none of them grew up as poor as he. Neither of Andrew's parents knew how to read or write. All schools charged tuition back then, and the Johnson family had little money. Andrew never went to school one day in his life.

Although the Johnsons were poor, Jacob and Mary did their best. Jacob worked as a bank porter, doing errands for the bank, and later served as a police officer. One winter day, he was hired as a porter for a boating party that included Thomas Henderson, publisher of the *Raleigh Star*. Henderson's boat capsized, and Jacob, on shore, jumped in Hunter's Mill Pond to rescue the publisher and his two friends. Thanks to Jacob's efforts, the three men survived. But a short time later, on January 4, 1812, Jacob Johnson died. It was just six days after Andrew's fourth birthday. Townspeople would later say Jacob's brave leap into the chilly water weakened his heart and led to his death.

Andrew Johnson's birthplace—behind Casso's Inn (center) *in Raleigh, North Carolina—was probably the small building to the left or right.*

Publisher Henderson printed an obituary (death announce-
ment) a week later, thanking Johnson for saving his life and
noted that Jacob was "esteemed for his honesty, sobriety,
industry, and his humane, friendly disposition."

The kind words may have soothed Mary and her children, but the family would face hard times and cruel
hunger. Elizabeth, Andrew's older sister, died during childhood. William was apprenticed to Henderson to learn the
printing trade. When the newspaperman died, William was
apprenticed to a tailor, James Selby.

LEARNING TO READ

Young Andrew liked visiting the tailor shop to see his brother William and to hear people reading to keep the apprentices' minds from wandering. By the time Andrew was
fourteen, he too was Selby's "bound boy," an apprentice.

Young men apprenticed to a tailor learned to sew and fashion clothing.

Most apprentices, like William, lived with their masters. But Andrew continued to live at home with his mother. The small amount of room-and-board money James Selby gave Andrew kept the boy and his mother from starving.

When Andrew was apprenticed, he began to learn to read. Shop manager James Litchford and one of the paid readers who visited the shop, Dr. William Hill, helped teach the teenager his ABCs. Andrew enjoyed the political speeches that Hill read and begged to borrow the book *The American Speaker.* Eventually, Hill gave Andrew the book, a collection of great British and American speeches. Andrew kept it with him his whole life. *The American Speaker* included essays on how to be a good speaker, and Andrew heeded those lessons. "Aim at nothing higher, till you can read distinctly and deliberately," the book counseled. "Learn to speak slow[ly], all other graces Will follow in the proper places."

Still, reading was a sideline. For twelve hours a day, Andrew and the other apprentices practiced the art of sewing. Andrew was good at it. Foreman Litchford remembered Andrew as "a wild harum-scarum boy with no unhonorable traits."

One Saturday night, when Andrew was fifteen, he, William, and two of their friends threw wood at a neighbor's house. No one knows why the four boys targeted Mrs. Wells's house. Maybe they didn't like Mrs. Wells, or maybe they did like her daughters. Mrs. Wells did not appreciate the attention. She threatened to get the boys in trouble with the law. They fled. Just by leaving Raleigh, the Johnsons were breaking the law. They were depriving James Selby of his apprentices. The impulsive actions of one night would change Andrew's life forever. Once he ran away, he would never live in his home state of North Carolina again.

The notice from June 1824 read: "Ten Dollars Reward." James Selby placed it in the local newspaper saying he'd pay what was then a good amount of money for the return of both brothers—or for Andrew alone. The tailor's ad cautioned others not to help or hire the Johnson boys. Apprentices like Andrew and William were bound to their masters, required to work for them without pay for years. The apprentice system gave tailors like Selby and other craftspeople free workers. In exchange, apprentices like Andrew and his brother learned a skill to support themselves. Apprentices were also supposed to be taught to read and write. Later, Andrew said that James Selby didn't live up to his part of the bargain since he never taught Andrew how to write.

After they ran away, the Johnson boys kept going for several days before stopping in Carthage, North Carolina, seventy-five miles from Raleigh. For a time, Andrew ran his own tailor shop out of a rented shack. Eventually, he moved to South Carolina, where he fell in love with a young woman named Mary Wood. Andrew made Mary a quilt and asked her to marry him, but Mary's mother didn't want her marrying a poor tailor. So Andrew left South Carolina. He went home to Raleigh to ask Selby to take him back. Under their contract, Andrew was supposed to stay apprenticed to the tailor until he turned twenty-one. But Selby was bitter and refused to accept the contrite eighteen-year-old. Andrew knew he would never find much work in a state where he was considered a runaway apprentice.

Ten Dollars Reward.

RAN AWAY from the Subscriber, on the night of the 15th instant, two apprentice boys, legally bound, named WILLIAM and AN DREW JOHNSON The former is of a dark complexion, black hair, eyes, and habits. They are much of a height, about 5 feet 4 or 5 inches The latter is very fleshy, freckled face, light hair, and fair complexion. They went off with two other apprentices, advertised by Messrs Wm. & Chas. Fowler When they went away, they were well clad—blue cloth coats, light colored homespun coats, and new hats, the maker's name in the crown of the hats, is Theodore Clark. I will pay the above Reward to any person who will deliver said apprentices to me in Raleigh, or I will give the above Reward for Andrew Johnson alone.

All persons are cautioned against harboring or employing said apprentices, on pain of being prosecuted.

JAMES J. SELBY, Tailor.

Raleigh, N. C. June 24, 1824   26 3t

According to James Selby's advertisement (above),
two other apprentices ran away with the Johnson brothers.

On a moonlit night, in August 1826, Andrew once again left Raleigh. He carried a bundle of his shirts and socks as he walked out of town, accompanied briefly by his friend Tom Lumsden. Lumsden remembered Andrew talking of all the great things he would accomplish in other places. But Lumsden knew his young friend was sad to have to leave home. "When he shook hands and bade me goodbye," Lumsden recalled, "[t]he tears just rolled down his cheeks."

Andrew traveled west to Columbia, Tennessee. He soon returned to Raleigh to rescue his mother and her second husband, Turner Doughty, who were close to starving. Andrew convinced them to leave Raleigh with him and head west to Sequatchie Valley, Tennessee. Andrew's brother and some of their mother's relatives lived there. Andrew and his elderly mother and stepfather didn't have money for a horse or carriage. Legend has it that a blind pony pulled a two-wheeled cart loaded with their few possessions. They walked by day, then slept under the stars. One night, what was probably a mountain lion dashed into camp, knocking their dinner into the fire.

"THERE GOES MY BEAU"

In September 1826, while on their way to Sequatchie Valley, Andrew and his family reached Greeneville, Tennessee. Andrew described it as "full of beauty and loveliness, honeysuckle and wild roses." The family decided to settle there, and Andrew went to work in a tailor shop. In the placid Scotch-Irish town of Greeneville, Andrew met dark-eyed Eliza McCardle.

The story goes that Eliza saw the tall, dark-haired newcomer walking down the street and told her friends, "There goes my beau [boyfriend]." Andrew soon fell in love with Eliza, who lived with her mother. Eliza's father, a shoemaker, was dead. In March 1827, when Greeneville's tailor retired, Andrew opened his own shop. Two months later, on May 17, 1827, eighteen-year-old Andrew married sixteen-year-old Eliza. He would be the only president to marry as a teenager. The young man who learned to read at fourteen and ran his own tailor shop did not know how to write his own name on the marriage certificate.

In the evenings, after Andrew was done sewing, Eliza taught him how to write and do simple math. He practiced his signature in the margins of his account books, but his spelling and writing skills would never be quite polished. Years later, when his secretary pointed out that Johnson had misspelled his own name, he had a quick comeback: "It is a man of small imagination who cannot spell his name more than one way."

Andrew Johnson cut high quality clothing with these tailor's shears.

CHAPTER TWO

AMBITIOUS TAILOR TO MECHANIC GOVERNOR

Some day I will show the stuck-up aristocrats who is running this country. A cheap purse-proud set they are, not half as good as the man who earns his bread by the sweat of his brow.

—Andrew Johnson

As the young couple began their family, Andrew Johnson's business—and ambition—grew. Johnson was used to hard work. He was proud of his sewing skills and said, "I always made a close fit . . . and did good work." For a reasonable fee—ten dollars—Johnson would sew a stylish suit of clothes, and soon the children of Greeneville sang a chant about the new tailor in town.

> *If you want a brand-new coat*
> *I'll tell you what to do:*
> *Go down to Andrew Johnson's shop*

And get a long tail blue
If you want the girls to love you,
To love you good and true,
Go down to Andy's tailor shop
And get a long tail blue.

While Johnson worked, Eliza sat beside him, reading aloud as he stitched. The teenagers had rented a small house that doubled as Johnson's shop. It was about ten feet square and had one bed, two or three stools, and Johnson's tailor platform, a small wooden area raised above the floor.

A year after they married, the Johnsons had their first child—Martha, born in 1828. Johnson's small business drew local men and students from the nearby college, who came because the tailor shop was a popular spot to talk politics. On Friday nights, the tailor who had never attended school would walk four miles to Greeneville College to take part in the local debating society. Soon Johnson was ready for his first public debate. He and another tradesman, a plasterer named Blackston McDaniel, debated whether the state of Tennessee should police the nearby Cherokee Indian territory. Johnson had formed strong ideas about many issues. He believed states had more power than the federal government. He argued that the Cherokee deserved to control their own land, just as states deserved the right to control themselves, rather than be controlled by the federal government.

In 1829 the twenty-year-old tailor was elected a town alderman. The following year, 1830, Eliza gave birth to their son, Charles, and Johnson won reelection. In 1831 the Johnsons bought their first house, on Water Street.

When Johnson bought his house on Water Street, he also bought this cabin for his tailoring business. The political debates moved there too.

◇

"Without a home," Johnson would say later, "there can be no good citizen, with a home, there can be no bad one."

Over the next few years, the Johnson family grew. Daughter, Mary, and son, Robert, were born. Johnson's ambition grew too. In 1834 Johnson joined the Tennessee Militia—the 19th Regiment—where he would earn the rank of colonel. That year he was also elected mayor of Greeneville and then state representative. For the next seven years, he would represent Greene and Washington counties at the state legislature in Nashville, Tennessee. In 1834 Johnson helped pass a new state constitution, which stated that citizens didn't need to own property to vote or hold office. Tennessee's new constitution opened the door for more poor white people to vote, but it also shut out

African Americans who weren't slaves. Slaves in Tennessee, like those around the country, did not have the right to vote. The new constitution, which passed by more than 70 percent, denied the voting rights of free black people as well.

Representative Johnson wasn't afraid to take unpopular stands. "Why, it would frighten horses!" was his rationale for opposing railroads. Johnson's unwillingness to spend public money to improve transportation cost him. In 1837 voters turned him out of office, angered because he didn't support better roads. But two years later, Johnson won election once again to the state legislature. He fought fellow lawmakers who wanted to open the legislature daily with a prayer. Johnson stood firm, noting that the U.S. Constitution called for a separation of church and state. He would later say he was not a religious man but did believe in God and the Bible. Eliza was raising the children as Methodists, but her husband refused to join any church. Johnson made it clear from the beginning that he believed that religion did not belong in government.

"HE TALKS STRONG THOUGHTS"

Johnson made a name for himself with his sharp speeches. His style was more ferocious than refined. A *New York Times* reporter wrote that Andrew Johnson's speeches "cut and slashed right and left, tore big wounds and left something behind to fester and remember. His phraseology may be uncouth but he talks strong thoughts and carefully culled facts in quick succession."

Johnson's stirring speeches and firm stands earned him enemies, including Parson William G. Brownlow, the editor of the *Jonesboro Whig* newspaper. Brownlow made his feelings clear in an October 28, 1840, editorial, headlined "Toady Alias Andrew Johnson." Brownlow would call Johnson "Toady Johnson" for years, but most others referred to Johnson as the colonel in deference to his militia rank.

The colonel's speeches gained a broader audience when he went to Washington, D.C., in 1843, as a Democratic congressman from Tennessee. Although 200 of the 223 members of Congress were lawyers, Representative Johnson didn't seem intimidated by his lack of education. He spoke forcefully on a range of issues from redistricting—redrawing the boundaries of election districts—to education and earned a reputation for extreme economy in government. Johnson voted against countless bills to spend government money. He

Andrew Johnson in 1842,
at age thirty-three
— ✧ —

opposed spending money for Washington, D.C., police and aqueducts, structures that bring fresh water into a city. He voted against aid to victims of the accidental explosion of a ship's cannon, which killed eight people including two cabinet officials.

One thing for which Andrew Johnson did believe in spending government money was education. He was passionate that schools should not be limited to those whose families had money. He was determined that his children would have the solid education he never had. By the time Johnson went to Washington, daughter Martha was old enough to go with him. She attended Mrs. English's Seminary and acted as his hostess. Eliza, who was sick with tuberculosis, stayed in Tennessee, caring for the younger children. Johnson lived at a boardinghouse but spent his free time reading history and politics at the Library of Congress. He kept mostly to himself and seldom attended the many social events that entertained other government officials. One of Johnson's contemporaries described his life as an "intense, unceasing, desperate, upward struggle."

Although Johnson became more successful as a tailor and politician, he never grew beyond his hatred for those born rich, whom he called the "stuck-up aristocrats." Yet Johnson himself became wealthy enough to afford slaves. He bought his first slave, a woman named Dolly, for five hundred dollars and later purchased her half-brother, Sam. Eventually, the Johnson family would own ten or eleven slaves, most of whom Johnson never sold. To Johnson, and to many white people of his time, African Americans were of an "inferior race—whose natural lot was one of dependency."

MAKE A POOR MAN REJOICE

No matter how many slaves he owned, no matter how much power he wielded in Washington, Andrew Johnson always considered himself a proud member of the working class. Back then, working-class people were called mechanics. They were tailors and cooks, tradesmen and day laborers. It was for those mechanics that Johnson, on March 27, 1846, first introduced his Homestead Bill.

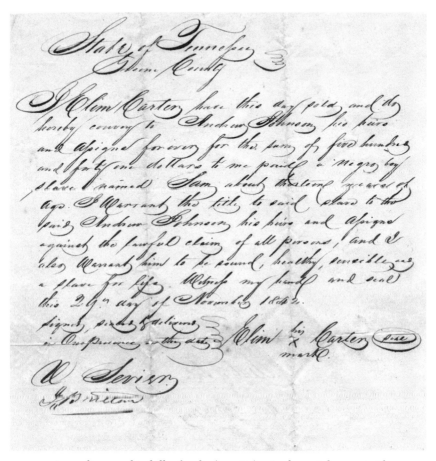

According to this bill of sale (receipt), Andrew Johnson paid $541 for a "boy slave named Sam about thirteen years of age" on November 29, 1842.

The idea was to encourage mechanics to help settle the West by giving 160 acres of public land to every poor white man who was the head of a household. Passing the Homestead Bill would "make many a poor man's heart rejoice," Johnson told his fellow lawmakers.

Famous British novelist Charles Dickens visited the U.S. Congress and described Andrew Johnson's looks as "remarkable . . . indicating courage, watchfulness, and certainly strength of purpose." And a May 1849 *New York Sunday Times* biographical sketch described Andrew as a "self-made man . . . of medium size and height; has a dark complexion, with black eyes and hair. His head is decidedly intellectual in shape, while from his eyes there flashes the fierce radicalism that burns in his soul."

In 1851 the Johnson family moved to a larger home in Greeneville, a two-story brick house on Main Street. (The house is part of the Andrew Johnson National Historic Site.) The following year, the Johnsons' last child, Andrew Jr. (nicknamed Frank), was born. Also that year, Andrew's stepfather died, and his mother moved in with the Johnsons and their five children.

✧ ————————————————
Johnson made a favorable impression on British novelist Charles Dickens (left).

*In 1851 the Johnsons moved to this two-story house
on Main Street in Greeneville.*

✧

The U.S. House of Representatives passed the Land Act, Johnson's Homestead Bill, in December 1852. The Senate and president still had to vote on the bill, but a crucial first obstacle was cleared. The bill would not become a law for many years.

After Johnson had served in Congress for ten years, his district in Tennessee was redrawn so it was divided into different voting districts. Those Democrats who might have voted for Johnson were unable to vote as a bloc (group) to keep him in power. The outspoken representative blamed his opponents in the Whig Party for intentionally chopping up his district. Johnson called it gerrymandering (when one political party reshapes a political district to break up another party's base of supporters). He was furious. "The

Whigs have cheated me out of Congress, they have torn the county of Greene from its sister counties, and attached it to a lot of foreign counties. They have split it up 'til it looks like a salamander. The fact is, they have 'gerrymandered' me out of Congress."

Losing his seat in Congress steered Johnson again toward state politics. In 1853 he decided to run for governor against Major Gustavus Henry, a man known as the "Eagle Orator." Johnson's opponent warned his supporters not to underestimate the tailor politician. "I have never met so powerful a speaker as Andrew Johnson," Henry said. In one debate, Henry charged that Johnson had been "heartless" to vote against sending money to Ireland, where the Great Potato Famine had killed hundreds of thousands of people. "When I voted against that resolution," Johnson responded, "I turned to my fellow congressmen and proposed to give fifty dollars of my own funds if they would give a like amount, and when they declined the proposition, I ran my hand in my pocket, Major Henry, and pulled out fifty dollars of good money, which I donated to the cause. How much did you give sir?"

On October 3, 1853, forty-four-year-old Andrew Johnson was elected governor of Tennessee. He would be known as the Mechanic Governor. Staying true to his roots while in office, he sewed a suit of clothes for the governor of Kentucky. The Kentuckian was a former blacksmith who, in thanks for the suit, sent Governor Johnson a handmade shovel and fireplace tongs. But no doubt Johnson's proudest moment as governor was the opening of Tennessee's first free public school and library. The uneducated runaway was doing his best to make sure other poor white people had a chance to learn and succeed.

*Tennessee voters elected Andrew Johnson to two terms
as governor, from 1853 to 1857.*

Two years later, Johnson ran for reelection against
Meredith P. Gentry, a member of the Know-Nothing Party,
whose platform called for ridding the country of Catholics
and foreigners. The Democratic governor said, "Show me a
Know-Nothing, and I will show you a loathsome reptile, on
whose neck every honest man should set his feet." When
members of his own political party asked Johnson to tone
down his speeches, the outspoken governor refused to yield:
"Gentlemen, I will make that same speech tomorrow if
it blows the Democratic party to hell." Johnson won
the election.

From the start, train travel was so much faster than horseback
or horse-drawn carriage that people put up with its dangers.

CHAPTER THREE

WAR

I am a Union man!
—Andrew Johnson

In 1857 the country was tense. Arguments over slavery fragmented the North, South, and West. The two-term governor of Tennessee wanted to be part of national politics once again. The Tennessee legislature named Johnson to the U.S. Senate. (At that time, U.S. senators weren't elected but were appointed by the state legislatures.)

On its way to the nation's capital, Johnson's train derailed, plunging sixty feet down an embankment. Johnson's arm was crushed near the elbow, and doctors needed to rebreak the shattered bone to set his arm. The injury would bother Johnson for years.

But a mangled limb couldn't destroy Johnson's elation. He told his fellow senators, "I have reached the summit of my ambition. The acme [high point] of all my hopes has been attained, and I would not give the position I occupy today for any other in the United States." Johnson intended to push colleagues to pass his beloved Homestead Bill, which most Southerners opposed. Southern states feared Northerners would settle the West and vote to make the new states that were created there free of slavery. In 1860 the United States had sixteen slave states plus two territories that allowed slaves, along with nineteen states and six territories that forbade slavery. If the West was settled and all the territories became states, Congress would be dominated by slave-free states. Maintaining an uneasy balance between free and slave states kept the capital on edge. As one senator noted, "Every Congressman is armed with a pistol or a bowie knife, some with both."

In May 1860, fourteen years after Johnson first proposed it, the Homestead Bill passed the Senate by a vote of forty-four to eight. But the measure still needed the president's approval to become law. Instead, President James Buchanan chose to veto it.

By fall, Johnson's attention was focused on a bigger issue than mechanics settling the West. He and others in Congress knew that the United States was poised for civil war. A Republican from Illinois—Abraham Lincoln—had been elected president. The South was angry that an anti-slavery man would be in the White House. In Congress, Senator Johnson delivered one of the most momentous speeches of his life. On December 18, 1860, the Southerner told the Senate he would stand by his country: "Let us exclaim that the Union, the Federal Union, it must be preserved!"

Major newspapers of the day, including the *New York Times* and *Chicago Tribune,* hailed Johnson's strong stand.

Letters and telegrams flooded the senator's office, calling him "a genuine patriot." But the stubborn Southerner also received death threats and was branded "a traitor to his section." Two days after Johnson's much-reported speech, South Carolina seceded from the Union. Johnson considered South Carolina's secession as treason. Tennesseans were divided. Those from eastern Tennessee, where Johnson and his family lived, owned few slaves and tended to support the Union. Johnson's longtime enemy, newspaper editor Parson Brownlow, began defending the man he had once labeled a "Toady." But western Tennessee and the state's governor Isham Green Harris backed the South. In Memphis, a crowd set a figure of Andrew Johnson on fire in protest.

─────────── ◇

Parson Brownlow

"LET THE BATTLE GO ON"

Shortly before dawn on April 12, 1861, just thirty-nine days after Lincoln's inauguration, Confederate troops opened fire on federal troops guarding Fort Sumter, a key fort in Charleston, South Carolina. The Civil War had begun. "We have commenced the battle of freedom," Johnson proclaimed, "I say, let the battle go on—until the Stars and Stripes shall again be unfurled upon every cross-road, and from every housetop."

Six Southern states followed South Carolina's lead in seceding from the Union. The country was divided. In Washington, Johnson gained fame and praise as the only

The Civil War started when Confederate (Southern) troops fired on Fort Sumter, South Carolina, in April 1861.

Southerner who stayed in Congress once war erupted. Before the war, he defended slavery and opposed abolitionists, who wanted to free the slaves. Johnson was comfortable with slavery, but he detested rich slave owners. He believed in the Union and the common man. Johnson told a Union general, "I am fighting those traitor aristocrats."

When Johnson went home to persuade Tennessee to stay in the Union, mobs stopped his train and tried to lynch him. Confederate president Jefferson Davis intervened. When an angry audience tried to shout him down at a church in Kingsport, Tennessee, Johnson drew a pistol from his pocket, set it on the pulpit, then calmly continued to speak. At least for a time, Johnson's fiery words swayed his state. But on June 8, 1861, Tennessee voted to secede. It was the eleventh and last state to leave the Union.

Johnson chose to stay in Washington. As the only loyal Southerner from a seceded state to remain in Congress, Johnson had President Lincoln's ear. Johnson begged for Union troops to reclaim his home state, which was under Confederate control. Eliza and the rest of Johnson's family were still living in Greeneville, surrounded by pro-slavery Confederates. Southern troops had taken over the Johnsons' home. "My wife and children have been turned into the street," Johnson protested, "And my house has been turned into a barrack, and for what? Because I stand by the Constitution. . . . This is my offense."

Union sympathizers in rebel-held Tennessee faced hard times. The Johnsons' oldest son, Charles, joined the Union

Johnson's son Charles served in the Union army.

✧ ————————————

army. Son Robert went into hiding. Martha's husband was arrested. Mary's husband was harassed. The Confederates took property and slaves from Union sympathizers. Eventually, Confederates gave Eliza permission to cross into Union territory to join her husband. The exhausting journey further weakened her. She never regained good health.

On March 4, 1862, after the Union captured Nashville, Lincoln named Andrew Johnson, the most famous loyal Southerner, military governor of Tennessee. The president told Johnson to "provide . . . peace and security to the loyal inhabitants of that state until they should be able to establish a civil government."

Strong-willed Johnson was probably harsher than Lincoln wanted. The new military governor promptly took a stand against those whom he saw as traitors to the Union. Johnson seized control of the Bank of Tennessee, shut down newspapers he considered disloyal, and arrested Nashville's mayor and several influential ministers for refusing to take a loyalty oath. The mayor, Richard B. Cheatham, dubbed Johnson's rule "a reign of terror.

But Johnson won praise for staying cool under intense pressure. In the fall of 1862, Confederate soldiers surrounded Nashville and seemed poised to recapture the Tennessee capital. Johnson prayed with a Methodist chaplain and vowed, "I am no military man, but anyone who talks of surrender, I will shoot."

————————— ✧
Johnson ruled with a firm hand as the military governor of Tennessee.

THE CIVIL WAR IN TENNESSEE

The Civil War started at Fort Sumter, South Carolina, but fighting soon spread. In the first year of the war, much of the action centered on Johnson's home state. Only Virginia would see more fighting than Tennessee. In February 1862, a Union general named Ulysses S. Grant captured two key Tennessee forts. Grant's victories at Fort Henry and Fort Donelson set the stage for a bloody battle at Pittsburg Landing, Tennessee. The battle became known as Shiloh, which was the name of a nearby church. Grant's army was camped at Pittsburg Landing, along the Tennessee River, waiting for more Union troops who would join them as they marched south to Mississippi. While Grant's troops waited, Confederates attacked.

Union general Ulysses S. Grant stayed close to the action during the Civil War, explaining, "The distant rear of an army engaged in battle is not the best place from which to judge correctly what is going on in front."

The Union army, under Grant, defeated the Confederates at Shiloh
in 1862 in one of the bloodiest battles of the Civil War.

On April 6 and 7, 1862, one of the most terrible battles of the war occurred. The Battle of Shiloh left about thirteen thousand Union soldiers dead, wounded, or missing. The South lost one-fourth of the Confederate soldiers who fought at Shiloh. The Confederate army was driven back south. Western Tennessee was back in Union hands.

Although most of the nation's people lived in the East, generals from both sides knew they had to control the West. "Whatever nation gets . . . control of the Ohio, Mississippi, and Missouri rivers, will control the continent," wrote Union general William Tecumseh Sherman. The South, which produced about three million bales of cotton each year but had almost no factories, depended upon rivers and railroads to export its raw cotton and bring in supplies. The Confederates' loss at Shiloh gave the Union control over a key Southern waterway, the Tennessee River.

The Confederates did not retake Nashville. The West remained under Union control. On May 20, 1862, President Lincoln signed the Homestead Act. The bill Andrew Johnson had first proposed sixteen years earlier became law. But it's doubtful Johnson had time to rejoice. The arm Johnson had injured in the train accident still hurt him. He worried about his family. Sons Charles and Robert both had drinking problems. Charles, a Union army surgeon, fell from a horse and died. Johnson was in Washington, D.C., and couldn't attend the funeral. Johnson wrote to Eliza, "I feel sometimes like giv[in]g up in dispare [despair]."

EMANCIPATION

On September 22, 1862, President Lincoln announced the Emancipation Proclamation. The proclamation said that "all persons held as slaves within any State, or designated part of a State, the people whereof shall then be in rebellion against the United States, shall be then, thenceforth, and forever free." The proclamation took effect January 1, 1863. Since the South ignored Union laws and Lincoln didn't include areas under Union military control, no slaves were freed. Yet the proclamation carried incredible weight, helping to convince Northerners that slaves would eventually gain their freedom.

In one way, Johnson's sentiments matched those of the president. Both men believed the preservation of the Union mattered more than their personal stands on slavery. Johnson had cast his lot with the Union and soon took an even bolder stance. On August 22, 1863, the man who said he would live and die believing slaves were inferior, spoke publicly, "I am for my Government with or without slavery, but if either the Government or slavery must perish, I say give me the Government and let the [slaves] go."

A FATEFUL NOMINATION

Abraham Lincoln was worried he would not be reelected. The Union army needed a victory to restore Northern hope. Lincoln decided to replace his vice president, a New Englander named Hannibal Hamlin, with a new running mate. He turned to the country's most famous Southern loyalist. Andrew Johnson said yes. People in Nashville roared their approval and cannons boomed. The Republican rail splitter from Illinois and the Democratic tailor from Tennessee were nominated by a new Republican Party, the Union Party. Cartoons mocked their modest backgrounds.

Neither Lincoln nor Johnson belonged to any particular church, yet many African Americans considered Lincoln and his new running mate their saviors. On October 24, 1864, shortly before the presidential election, Johnson told a crowd of former slaves outside the state capitol, "I will indeed be your Moses [the biblical figure who led Israelites out of slavery in Egypt], and lead you through the Red Sea of war and bondage to a fairer future of liberty and peace."[20] Abraham Lincoln and Andrew Johnson won the election in 1864. But the year would end on a sad note for the Johnson family. In December, Mary's husband died in battle.

Lincoln and Johnson greet guests at the inaugural ball in 1865.

CHAPTER FOUR

VICE PRESIDENT, THEN PRESIDENT

Andy ain't a drunkard.
—Abraham Lincoln

March 4, 1865, brought a great moment in Johnson's life. The dark, rainy day marked his first inauguration, and Lincoln's second. But Johnson was sick. Some say he had typhoid fever. The trip from Tennessee to Washington, D.C., had left him exhausted. The night before and the morning of the inauguration, Johnson drank a lot of whiskey. At the ceremony, he appeared to be drunk and made a foolish speech, which shocked the high-level audience and gave the newspapers reason to scorn the tailor turned vice president. After Johnson's embarrassing ramble, Lincoln stood and delivered one of his most impressive speeches about the war, saying, "With malice towards none; with charity for all; with firmness in the right as God gives us to see the right, let us strive on to finish the work we are in."

The contrast between the eloquent president and his new vice president seemed striking. Lincoln tried to defend Johnson, telling an advisor, "I have known Andy Johnson for many years; he made a bad slip the other day, but you need not be scared; Andy ain't a drunkard." Johnson would never appear drunk in public again, but the damage was done. Newspapers mocked "Andy the Sot [drunk]." The vice president was ignored. He did not attend meetings of the cabinet, a group of the president's advisors, and he was rarely invited to the White House. He would not meet privately with the president again for a month.

The war, which had dragged on for more than four years, was nearing its end. After the Union captured the Confederate capital of Richmond, Virginia, on April 2, 1865, Lincoln and Johnson toured the ruined city together. On April 9, Confederate general Robert E. Lee surrendered

to Union general Ulysses S. Grant. The war was nearly over. The people in the North were ecstatic. Lincoln's attention, like that of the nation, had been focused on war, not how the country would be rebuilt. No one knew what Lincoln's plan to rebuild the South would look like. "My

✧ ————————————

Just a month after taking office as vice president, Johnson joined Lincoln on a tour of Richmond, Virginia. There was little to see but rubble.

policy," the president said, "is to have no policy." Lincoln's political gift was in being flexible and adapting to what was happening. No one seemed to care what the vice president thought. Johnson told Charles Dana, a War Department assistant, that Southerners should be allowed back into the Union only under certain conditions and with some penalties. Dana suggested the vice president talk to the president. But since the inauguration, Lincoln had mostly ignored Johnson.

On April 11, Lincoln gave a hint of what he was thinking when he spoke to a crowd outside the White House. He spoke in favor of the right to vote for African Americans who were educated or owned land. On April 14, Lincoln told a cabinet meeting that the federal government couldn't run each state government. Instead, people in those

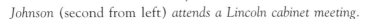

Johnson (second from left) attends a Lincoln cabinet meeting.

Southern states would have to be responsible for leading their states well. That same day, Johnson visited the White House to complain to Lincoln that General Grant's peace terms with Confederate general Robert E. Lee were too generous.

That night Lincoln and his wife Mary went to Ford's Theatre. While the president celebrated the war's end, Johnson slept in his room at the Kirkwood Hotel. A loud banging on his hotel room door awakened him. Former Wisconsin governor Leonard J. Farwell shouted that he had to see Johnson. Farwell told the vice president that Lincoln had been shot at Ford's Theatre. Secretary of State William Seward had been stabbed and seriously wounded at his home. Johnson, in shock, refused to be escorted by troops and instead went with Farwell and a military policeman to visit Lincoln as he lay dying. After seeing

———————————— ✧ ————————————

Johnson (third from right, standing) *squeezes into the room where Lincoln lay dying.*

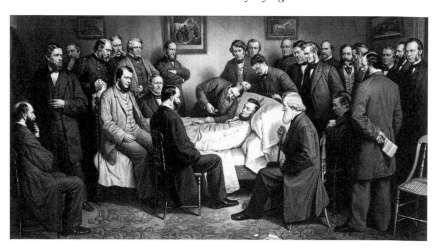

*Johnson (fourth from left) takes the oath of office
in the Kirkwood Hotel lobby on April 15, 1865.*

the mortally wounded president, Johnson returned to his
hotel, saying, "They [Southerners] shall suffer for this.
They shall suffer for this." The next day, April 15, 1865,
at 7:22 A.M., Lincoln died. A few hours later, Chief
Justice Salmon P. Chase administered the oath of office to
Johnson in the lobby of the Kirkwood Hotel. After only
forty-one days as vice president, Andrew Johnson had
become president of the United States.

Johnson held his first cabinet meeting at the hotel at
noon, just hours after Lincoln's death. The stunned new
leader told cabinet officials gathered around him, "I feel
incompetent to perform duties so important and responsible as those which have been so unexpectedly thrown
upon me."

Johnson became president on April 15, but he didn't move into the White House until May, to give Mrs. Lincoln and her family time to move. Later, Eliza and the rest of the family moved in. Eventually, the couple's two remaining sons, two daughters, one son-in-law, and five grandchildren lived there.

After Lincoln's death, sightseers had ripped up the White House furnishings for souvenirs. Because Eliza was still ill, Martha restored the residence on a limited budget while her father worked to reconstruct the country. She woke early each morning to milk the cows that pastured on the White House lawn. "We are plain people from the mountains of Tennessee, called here for a short time by calamity," Martha said. "I trust too much will not be expected of us." Martha and the rest of the Johnson family found that much was expected of those who live in the White House.

David Trotter Patterson

Martha was not only the White House hostess for her father, but also the wife of a U.S. senator, David Trotter Patterson. She felt the pressure of living in such a public role and told a reporter, "If I could only walk about a little with my children sometimes in the grounds without being stared at, and really enjoy the comfort of an old dress and a little privacy."

Andrew Johnson, too, probably had little privacy. The man who had a reputation for always being well groomed and well dressed knew the eyes of the nation were on him. A painful war followed by the country's first assassination shook the United States. Johnson tried to do his best to restore the nation.

On May 23, 1865, the U.S. flag flew high again for the first time since Lincoln's death. The country was honoring the heroes of the Grand Armies of the Republic. For two days, Union troops marched through Washington in a giant victory parade. Peace seemed to be at hand. But the president faced the difficult task of rebuilding a torn country.

Johnson watches the Union victory parade from this viewing stand.

TOUGH ACT TO FOLLOW

Abraham Lincoln, who had been ridiculed and criticized in life, received endless adoration in death. Many Americans had dismissed the gangly Illinois lawyer as slow to act, a backwoods politician who waffled rather than taking definitive stands. But after his assassination, Lincoln was recognized as a great leader whose strength lay in being willing to compromise when necessary. Americans began comparing Lincoln to George Washington. It was a dramatic turnaround from just months before, when Lincoln had been compared to an ape. The funeral train carrying Lincoln's body home to Springfield, Illinois, traveled for fourteen days. Along the way, thousands of mourners waited hours in line to say good-bye to the slain president.

Of course, not everyone worshiped the memory of Lincoln. A group called the Radical Republicans had been disgusted by Lincoln's moderate approach. They wanted universal suffrage (right to vote) and equal rights for all African Americans immediately. And they wanted the South to be punished. After Lincoln's death, one Radical Republican wrote, "The universal feeling among Radical men is that his [Lincoln's] death is a godsend."

Johnson was suddenly responsible for a country exhausted and embittered by war. The Civil War had killed about 620,000 people, seriously wounded 500,000 soldiers, and ravaged enormous stretches of the South. It would be up to a Southerner who sided with the North to shape the peace. Abolitionist George Stearns told Johnson, "Today you occupy a position more potent for good or evil than any man on the face of the earth."

The new president also had to deal with doubts about the assassination conspiracy. Some Americans believed Johnson, a Southerner, had a role in the plot to kill the president. Lincoln's assassin, John Wilkes Booth, had left a message for Johnson at his hotel on April 14. The message read, "Don't wish to disturb you. Are you at home? J. Wilkes Booth." It's unclear whether Johnson got the note or knew who Booth was before the shooting. But Booth's conspiracy had included plans to kill Johnson. Another Booth conspirator, carriage maker George Atzerodt, had a room at the same hotel as Johnson. Atzerodt was supposed to kill the vice president but lost his nerve.

✧ ——————————

George Atzerodt, photographed in prison, was involved in the failed plot to kill Johnson.

Johnson, like Secretary of War Edwin Stanton, believed Confederate leaders were behind the conspiracy to kill Lincoln. No evidence ever linked Confederate president Jefferson Davis to the plot, but hundreds of people were arrested, including eight who were quickly tried before a military court. George Atzerodt, two other men, and one woman were sentenced to death. They were hanged on July 7, 1865, less than three months after Lincoln's death. The president's killer, John Wilkes Booth, never stood trial. On April 26, Booth was shot in the head by a Union sergeant at a Virginia barn where federal troops had trapped the fleeing assassin.

"WE HAVE FAITH IN YOU"

Although some Northerners believed Johnson had a role in the assassination plot, many others were optimistic that the country's new Southern president could lead the country into peace. Radical Republicans, such as Ohio senator Benjamin Franklin Wade, who believed passionately in equal rights for African Americans, were excited about the new president. "Johnson, we have faith in you," Wade told him. "By the Gods, there will be no trouble in running the government."

In the beginning, President Johnson seemed to please most sides. As strong-minded as the Mechanic Statesman was, it was not easy to know his thoughts. He never kept a diary and rarely wrote letters. Navy secretary Gideon Wells said Johnson "has no confidants and seeks none" and that most of his major decisions seem to be made without consulting with "anyone whatsoever."

Within weeks of Lincoln's death, President Johnson began to act. He overruled Union general William

Sherman's peace plan with Confederates in Georgia, calling it too soft. On May 29, 1865, Johnson proclaimed pardons for most Southerners who would agree to sign a loyalty oath to the Union. And he signed the first plan to restore the South—a blueprint for how to bring North Carolina back into the Union. The new commander in chief considered trying Confederate general Robert E. Lee for treason, but Union general Ulysses Grant threatened to resign if Johnson arrested Lee. Johnson gave up this idea.

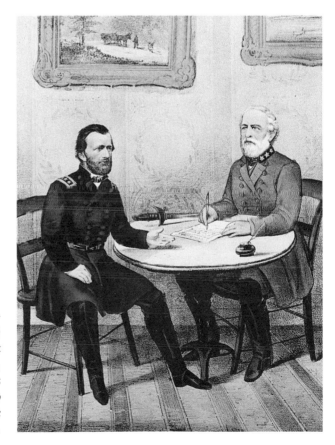

After Lee (right) surrendered to Grant (left) on April 12, 1865, Grant used his power as a war hero to protect Lee from punishment.

CHAPTER FIVE

PRESIDENTIAL RECONSTRUCTION

White men alone must manage the south.
—Andrew Johnson

Andrew Johnson faced an almost impossible job. He was in charge of rebuilding a country torn apart by four years of war. This postwar time became known as Reconstruction, since much of the country was being rebuilt, or reconstructed. At first, Johnson had more control over Reconstruction than anyone else.

The new president had one advantage over Lincoln. Since Johnson was a Southerner, it was probably easier for other Southerners to work with him, rather than with a Northerner like Lincoln. One supporter from Tennessee wrote, "Our Southern brothers are beginning to know that you are their friend, their protector, and to feel that in thy hands a nation's fate lies." Still, many people in the South regarded President Johnson as a traitor to their cause.

Somehow, Johnson had to convince fellow Southerners to accept that they were truly part of the United States.

Eleven states had seceded, but to Johnson, they had never left the Union. He firmly believed secession violated the Constitution, so it was illegal for any state to secede. The new president saw the Constitution as a solid document that could never be broken. He believed the Constitution outlined how the country was meant to be governed, and what was written in that document could not be changed. Secession wasn't mentioned in the Constitution. Therefore, states simply couldn't legally secede. His goal was to bring the South back into the United States as quickly as possible—and to help poor whites rather than rich plantation owners or former slaves.

◊

This cartoon criticizes Johnson for delaying Reconstruction with a lot of talk but little action. Columbia (left), holding a child, represents the United States. She wants Johnson (right) to hurry up and fix the South, represented by a big, leaky teakettle. Johnson is carrying the tools to make the repairs.

MENDING THE FAMILY KETTLE.

COLUMBIA—" *Now, Andy, I wish you and your boys would hurry up that job, because I want to use that kettle right away. You are all talking too much about it.*"

THE STATE OF THE NATION

By the end of the war, half a million soldiers were left
seriously injured. Many had lost arms or legs. Cities and
towns sponsored penmanship contests to encourage soldiers
to practice writing with their only remaining hand. In 1865
Mississippi spent 20 percent of its total state budget on
artificial limbs for maimed soldiers. Many Northern soldiers
ended up addicted to morphine, a drug that had been used
as a painkiller in military hospitals. The South didn't have
enough money to give its injured soldiers morphine.

Although civilians and soldiers from both sides suffered,
the South faced many more problems. The Union army had
burned and destroyed the land in large sections of the South.
Union soldiers demolished five miles of Southern railroad
a day. The war destroyed ten billion dollars' worth of
Southern property.

✧ ————————

*In this postwar view of
a Richmond, Virginia,
railroad depot, a locomotive
and the railroad tracks
are damaged almost
beyond recognition.*

But property damage accounted for only part of the South's loss. One of every five white men in the South died because of the war. Hunger further weakened Southerners. After the war, about ten thousand former Confederates refused to live in the re-United States. They chose to immigrate to other countries. A popular lithograph entitled "The Lost Cause" (below) portrayed the mood of the South. The lithograph showed a weary soldier dragging himself home, only to see his homestead in ruins, the gravestones of his family askew. President Johnson was responsible for rebuilding this dispirited, exhausted country. Reconstruction would not be easy.

Johnson hoped poor whites would gain some of the plantation owners' former lands and power. But he feared that former slaves would receive preference over the poor white people. He decided that the only people in the South who could keep African Americans under control were their former owners. He made sure that wealthy Southerners were excluded from the general amnesty he had declared in the spring. Instead, to have their rights restored, the rich landowners had to apply to the president for individual pardons. The man who had grown up poor and at the mercy of rich Southerners seemed to enjoy the presidential power he held over the people he grew up hating. But Johnson was easy on the landowners. He granted pardons— and returned land—to almost all the plantation owners who appealed to him. What's more, Johnson allowed those plantation owners and former Confederate leaders to once again run for office and represent the South. Four Confederate generals, five colonels, and the Confederacy's vice president were all elected to Congress after the war. Northerners in Congress refused to recognize what they saw as illegal Southern congressmen. Northern lawmakers controlled Congress, so the South ended up without representation when the congressmen it had elected weren't recognized as valid members of Congress.

A RACIST PRESIDENT

In Johnson's mind, African Americans had no part in Reconstruction. The future of millions of freed slaves hinged on a Southern president with deeply racist beliefs. Johnson's private secretary wrote that the president "exhibited a morbid distress and feeling against [African

Americans]." The Tennessean resisted efforts to help freed slaves, saying, "This is a country for white men, and by God, as long as I am president, it shall be a government for white men." That white government received many appeals for help, such as this letter from a Georgia freed-man: "While southern people were carrying on an awful rebellion the colored people was bleeding and dying for the Union. While the southern people was trying to break the Constitution the colored people was for the Union. We have done all we can. We now look to you for help."

———————————— ✧ ————————————

Thousands of freed and escaped slaves had eagerly served in Union regiments during the Civil War.

The White House ignored freed slaves' pleas for help. Johnson said the government never gave poor whites any special breaks. Therefore, poor blacks shouldn't get any either. The president wasn't optimistic that freed slaves could thrive in the United States. He told a group of African Americans that they might be better off moving to another country. "The time may soon come when you shall be gathered together in a clime [climate] and country suited to you, should it be found that the two races cannot get along together."

Northerners who had hoped the end of the Civil War would bring full citizenship to African Americans were devastated. One wrote to Johnson, "You . . . had . . . a grand opportunity to settle the [African American] question . . . and you missed it." Abolitionists were outraged when the president allowed Confederates to vote but would not agree to grant voting rights to African American soldiers who had helped in the Union victory.

Instead of enjoying full freedom, former slaves were forced to live by Black Codes, laws that limited their rights. Every state in the South passed some kind of Black Codes. These laws restricted where African Americans could live, work, and travel. The biased codes gave whites almost total power. Whites had the power to auction off blacks who weren't working or were traveling without permission. African Americans who wanted any kind of job but fieldwork had to get permission from a white judge. African American children were taken from their parents and forced into apprenticeships. The postwar South was far from gentle with freed slaves. One observer in Louisiana said whites "govern by the pistol and the rifle." Many Northerners were outraged. They wanted the president to overturn the Black Codes. Johnson insisted that states had rights that the federal government could not supersede, or cancel.

Many Northerners insisted that the South had to change. Radical Republicans and others wanted a new amendment to the Constitution. They proposed the Thirteenth Amendment, which states that "neither slavery nor involuntary servitude . . . shall exist in the United States." Although he had opposed slavery, the president refused to support the amendment. Johnson claimed the Constitution did not need to be amended. He believed the states, rather than the federal government, should decide such issues. Congress and many Northerners disagreed.

FAMILY LIFE IN THE WHITE HOUSE

By summer's end, Johnson was sick, at least in part because of overwork. His schedule was exhausting. He got up at six o'clock and read the papers with Eliza. She then went through countless more newspapers and reported the highlights to him at breakfast the next morning. Johnson worked in his White House office from nine to four o'clock. After dinner he went for a walk or carriage ride. Then Johnson went back to the office to meet with visitors from nine to eleven o'clock. He had a telegraph office set up in the White House and also installed the first White House barber's chair. This president believed in spending long days at work.

The entire Johnson family lived at the White House. When his five grandchildren had first arrived in August 1865, the president ran outside and squatted down to hug them all. Johnson's daughters, Martha and Mary, each named a son in honor of the president. So five-year-old

Andrew and eight-year-old Andrew played with their grandfather, as did their sisters—six-year-old Belle, seven-year-old Sarah, and ten-year-old Lillie. Playing with his grandchildren gave Johnson a chance to relax. His bodyguard, Colonel William Crook, recalled, "Although his life of fighting for principles had developed him into a stern, forbidding, uncompromising man . . . when he was with his . . . grandchildren he relaxed . . . into . . . a genial [friendly], happy man for the hour—until official duties called him away from his family circle."

Johnson's family circle held disappointments as well as joy. Eliza's tuberculosis kept her mostly upstairs in her room. Daughters Martha and Mary acted as official White House hostesses in their mother's place. Robert, who

✧ ——————————

Eliza McCardle Johnson

worked as one of his father's personal secretaries, created gossip with his excessive drinking. Rumors circulated that Robert brought prostitutes into the White House. Johnson decided to send his hard-drinking son to Africa to report on conditions there, but Robert disappeared on a drinking binge instead. He remained in Washington, helping—and hindering—his father.

Despite the disappointments and pressures, President Johnson tried his best to move the country from war to peace quickly. In the first six months after the war's end, some eight hundred thousand of the Union's nearly one million soldiers were discharged. Europe and Mexico had feared that the United States would maintain its huge army and grab more land, but Andrew Johnson did not want more war. The president, like much of the country, was hungry for peace.

Martha Johnson Patterson

The Civil War changed how Americans thought of their country. Before the war, people had said, "The United States are . . . ," but after the war, the phrase shifted to "the United States is. . . . " The country was on its way to being one united union of states, but the path to unity was difficult. The president did what he thought best. He tried to be generous, rather than punitive, to most of the people, although he was far from generous to freed slaves. Still, one major historian, Henry Steele Commager, would later write, "No other civil war ever concluded with so little punishment or so much generosity as that of the Union and Confederacy."

Johnson believed the country was getting back together. On October 13, 1865, he declared, "We are making very rapid progress—so rapid I sometimes cannot realize it. It appears like a dream!"

That same month, Johnson's brother, William, who had run away with him decades earlier, shot himself unintentionally while hunting and died. In November one of the president's longtime friends, Preston King, became overwhelmed by depression and drowned himself. In his first year as president, Johnson endured countless struggles, both personal and political.

Johnson's stands on the Black Codes and the Thirteenth Amendment alienated many moderate and radical Republicans. But by autumn 1865, he had gained support from conservative Republicans and white Southerners, many of whom were Democrats. The president wanted to unite his conservative supporters. But his strategy to ignore moderate Republicans was risky, as publisher Joseph Medill warned: "They (Republicans) control twenty states and both branches of Congress. Four-fifths of the soldiers sym-pathize with them. Can you afford to quarrel with . . . mil-lions of voters?" Andrew Johnson, as dogged as ever, refused to bend.

On December 4, 1865, the president sent his first State of the Union message to Congress. He announced that "the work of Reconstruction" was complete. Congress disagreed. The tension between the White House and Republican-controlled Congress swelled. On December 18, the Thirteenth Amendment was ratified by three-fourths of the states and became law. The amendment made slavery unconstitutional. Republicans were delighted. Congress began its own version of Reconstruction, leaving Johnson powerless in the White House.

CHAPTER SIX

A "DEAD DOG" PRESIDENT

*Give my respects to the dead dog
of the White House.*

—Tennessee governor Parson Brownlow,
referring to Andrew Johnson

More than six months after Johnson became president, he hosted his first White House reception—an 1866 New Year's Day celebration. But the president had little reason to feel cheerful. He faced growing pressure from Congress, especially from the Radical Republicans. The Radicals were angry that Johnson wouldn't give African Americans equal rights. He refused to compromise. This hurt his standing among moderates in Congress, whom he needed if he were going to have any influence in Congress.

Johnson seemed unaware of the give-and-take of politics. He remained headstrong, surly, and suspicious. He alienated those middle-of-the-road lawmakers, the congressional moderates, who could have helped him.

This cartoon criticizes Johnson's use of the presidential veto to limit the rights of freedmen, or former slaves. He symbolically kicks the Freedmen's Bureau down a flight of stairs. This government agency helped freedmen adapt to freedom.

——————————— ✧

VETOES AND OVERRIDES

On February 19, 1866, Johnson vetoed a bill to continue the Freedmen's Bureau. Johnson believed the South "would treat the [African American] with greater kindness than the [N]orth if it were left alone and not exasperated [annoyed]." To him, the Freedmen's Bureau was "little better than another form of slavery." The president also wanted to make the point that Congress should not make laws affecting the South until the South was represented in Congress. Northerners still refused to recognize many of the South's congressmen. Northerners claimed the elections were not valid because former Confederate officials weren't allowed to serve in Congress. Johnson's Freedmen's Bureau veto thrilled southern Democrats. One Democratic newspaper trumpeted this headline: "ALL HAIL! GREAT AND GLORIOUS! GREAT VICTORY FOR THE WHITE MAN."

FREEDMEN'S BUREAU

"I felt like a bird out of a cage," said one slave, Houston Holloway, upon hearing that the Civil War had ended. "Amen. Amen. Amen. I could hardly ask to feel any better than I did on that day." But freedom alone would not be enough for Holloway and some four million other former slaves.

In March 1865, Congress set up the Freedmen's Bureau to "devise a new social order between freedmen [former slaves] and former masters." The bureau was supposed to help African Americans adjust to being free. The war had freed the slaves, but it had destroyed the land they and their former owners lived on. The cities of the South had been burned, railroads wrecked, and farm fields abandoned. Southerners—white and black—needed help rebuilding their society. Both blacks and whites needed to learn new roles, new ways to live together. As slaves, African Americans had no rights and no education but received at least minimal food and shelter. After the war, as freedmen, African Americans had some rights but desperately needed education and jobs so they could pay for their own food and shelter. Because of the war, many whites also lacked the same basic needs. They resented the freed slaves for destroying their way of life. The bureau could do little to protect freedmen from whites' hatred. In 1866 a bureau agent wrote with frustration about how "a freedman is now standing at my door, his tattered clothes bespattered with blood from his head caused by blows inflicted by a white man with a stick and we can do nothing for him."

Agents from the Freedmen's Bureau set up schools so former slaves could learn to read and write. Northerners went South to volunteer as teachers. But the bureau itself never had enough money. One South Carolina bureau agent, for example, was responsible for forty thousand former slaves.

The Freedmen's Bureau could do little when whites took violent action against African Americans.

─────────────── ✧ ───────────────

President Johnson did not support the Freedmen's Bureau. He believed Southern states could handle problems without being forced to obey a Northern-run federal agency. Johnson wanted states, not the federal government, to solve state problems. The Freedmen's Bureau's job was made more difficult by the president's hostile attitude toward its work. "I fear you have Hercules's [a mythic Greek hero's] task," wrote General Sherman to General O. O. Howard, commissioner of the new bureau.

Howard wanted to give each freedman a small, forty-acre plot of land from the almost one million acres of abandoned land in the South. "Forty acres and a mule" became a popular rallying cry among former slaves. But the plan failed. President Johnson chose to return the abandoned property to the former white owners. Blacks would not get a chance to own land. Instead, they had to rent land from whites, some of whom were their former owners. Freedmen paid a portion of what they grew as rent. The freed slaves had become sharecroppers, sharing their crops with their former masters.

The bureau did succeed in helping to educate African Americans. Four years after the war ended, the bureau had set up three thousand schools for 150,000 former slaves. By then, black teachers who had been trained by the bureau began to outnumber white teachers. When the Freedmen's Bureau was officially closed in 1872, 20 percent of the freed slaves could read. African Americans' education would continue to improve. By 1910, 70 percent of African Americans were able to read.

◆

Classes are in session at the Freedmen's Bureau in Richmond, Virginia.

Northerners were angry. The same day that the president vetoed the Freedmen's Bureau, Congress overrode him. Every moderate in Congress joined the Radical Republicans in voting to keep the Freedmen's Bureau, despite the president's opposition. Two days later, on Washington's birthday, outside the White House, an angry Johnson stunned a large crowd with a long-winded, fiery speech about the Radical Republicans. He claimed they were "laboring to destroy the fundamental principles of government." The president had lost the power to

✧
Johnson delivers a passionate speech from the White House steps.

control the way the country was governed by refusing to work with Congress.

A month later, Congress passed the Civil Rights Act, which outlawed the South's discriminatory Black Codes and also ensured that African Americans born in the United States were citizens. This act, the first measure to define citizens' rights, declared, "all persons born in the United States . . . without regard to any previous servitude shall have the same rights in every State and Territory." The Civil Rights Act gave citizens the right to sue, make contracts, and buy and sell property.

The act did not say anything about African Americans' right to vote. Nor did it mention the civil rights of women. Women such as Susan B. Anthony and Elizabeth Cady Stanton were so disappointed that they formed the National Woman Suffrage [voting] Association, which campaigned for women's right to vote. A new movement for civil rights was born.

If President Johnson had signed the Civil Rights Act into law, he would have won the support of moderates and divided Republicans in Congress. Instead, Johnson chose to once again use his presidential veto power. He insisted that the act went against "all our experience as a people. . . . The distinction of race and color is by the bill made to operate in favor of the colored and against the white race." On April 9, moderate and Radical Republicans joined to overturn the president's veto. Johnson was furious. He said Congress was filled with traitors. Newspapers that favored the Radical Republicans called the president an "insolent [overbearing], drunken brute." Two of the country's three branches of government—Congress and the White House—were deadlocked.

THE RADICAL REPUBLICANS

The Radical Republicans were a minority in their party—extremists who demanded immediate rights for freed slaves and punishment for the Confederate South. Three senators and one representative made up the heart of the Radicals.

Representative Thaddeus Stevens of Pennsylvania was the Radicals' leader. Long before the Civil War, Stevens had already cared deeply about African Americans' rights. He was born poor, and a deformed foot and leg caused him to limp badly. He was handsome when he was young. By the time Johnson reached the White House, Stevens was in his seventies, a gaunt, stern man who knew how to get things done in Congress.

Massachusetts senator Charles Sumner also had a passion for black suffrage. But Sumner didn't have Stevens's skills in public speaking. The Bostonian was famous for his long-winded speeches. Senators Zachariah Chandler of Michigan and Benjamin Franklin Wade of Ohio were also devoted to African Americans' rights.

Thaddeus Stevens

———— ◇ ————

At first, the Radical Republicans thought Johnson would be on their side. They had considered Lincoln too wishy-washy, always seeking the middle ground instead of pushing hard to free the slaves. But within Johnson's first year as president, the Radical Republicans realized this Southerner was not their ally. So they began doing everything they could to damage the stubborn president's reputation. It's hard to say who was less willing to compromise—the president or the Radical Republicans.

THE CRUEL UNCLE AND THE VETOED BABES IN THE WOOD.

The Civil Rights Act marked the first time Congress overturned a presidential veto of major legislation. The thirty-three to fifteen vote to override his veto showed the country how little power the president had left. Yet Johnson appeared confident, almost unaware he was losing political power. He told his private secretary, "Sir, I am right. I know I am right and I am damned if I do not adhere to it."

Johnson's Civil Rights veto cost him dearly. The *Chicago Tribune,* which earlier had praised the Southerner who stayed loyal to the Union, endorsed impeachment, which is the way Congress can fire a president for wrongdoing in office. That spring, Alfred E. Burr, editor of the Democratic *Hartford Times,* wrote, "The Democratic voters, to a man, are with him. The Republican voters, by a large majority, are against him. Unite all the friends of the President, and he will carry all of the Northern states, or at least a majority of them. But if he depends on his friends in the Republican party, and on those only, he will certainly be defeated at every point." The president had to try to work with both moderate and liberal Democrats and Republicans. He needed supporters from both parties if he was going to have much political power.

Yet Johnson refused to compromise with moderate Republicans, who ended up working with the Radical Republicans. By the end of his term, Johnson set a record for vetoes—rejecting twenty-nine bills. Congress managed to override fifteen of them.

Republicans spread rumors that Johnson was power mad and had been part of the plot to kill Lincoln. A committee of congressmen took a year to look into President Johnson's bank accounts. He was furious. He told his secretary, "I have had a son killed, a son-in-law die during the last battle of Nashville, another son has thrown himself away, a second son-in-law is in no better condition, I think I have had enough sorrow without having my bank account examined by a Committee of Congress."

An illness added to the president's problems. In late winter and early spring 1866, he suffered from a painful bout of kidney stones. But by April, the kidney stones had passed and the president recovered. Johnson called his illness "the gravel." No doubt the gravel or kidney stones were at least part of the reason the president rarely smiled.

RACIST ATTITUDES AND ACTIONS

On May 1, 1866, a fight in Memphis, Tennessee, between black and white carriage drivers turned into a three-day race riot. Forty-six people died in the riot—all but two of whom were African Americans. The massacre targeted those African Americans who had just left the Union army.

People with rifles take aim at fleeing African Americans during the Memphis riots of 1866. Buildings burn in the background.

Later that month, Congress passed the Fourteenth Amendment to the Constitution, which guaranteed that African Americans were citizens of the United States and the state in which they live. The amendment, which forbade states from depriving any citizen of equal protection under the law, was a major step forward in the federal government's power over the states. The measure also banned former Confederates from holding state or federal office.

Johnson strongly opposed the bill and was willing to spend twenty thousand dollars of his own money to defeat it. He tried to create a new political party—the National Union Convention—to block it. The president urged all Southerners, especially those in his home state, to reject the amendment. From Washington, Johnson did what he could to stop Tennessee from ratifying the amendment. But Governor Parson Brownlow, Johnson's longtime opponent, threatened to arrest Tennessee lawmakers who refused to show up to vote. Brownlow triumphed and sent a telegram to the senate clerk, boasting: "We have fought the battle and won it. We have ratified the Constitutional Amendment in the House. . . . Give my respects to the dead dog of the White House."

On July 30, 1866, another race riot erupted, this time in New Orleans, Louisiana. The police, mostly Confederate veterans, shot into a crowd of African Americans, leaving forty-eight people dead. The president's lack of response after the massacres, coupled with his vetoes, enraged those who wanted him to help the freed slaves. Still, civil rights supporters had little choice but to try to persuade the president to consider African Americans' rights. Senator Charles Sumner of Massachusetts spent hours trying to sway the president. When Sumner reached for his hat to leave the White House, he realized that Johnson had used it as a spittoon and had spit tobacco juice into it.

Noted African American editor Frederick Douglass also met with President Johnson at the White House. Afterward, the president insulted the respected black reformer, saying Douglass was "just like any [African American], and he would sooner cut a white man's throat than not."

Charles Sumner (left) *and Frederick Douglass* (right) *both experienced Johnson's scorn for supporting the Fourteenth Amendment.*

Johnson's racist attitude toward African Americans mirrored that of many Southerners. The Ku Klux Klan was founded in 1866 in Pulaski, Tennessee. Former Confederate general Nathan Bedford Forrest became the Klan's first grand dragon, or leader. Klansmen disguised themselves under white sheets that supposedly represented the ghosts of rebel soldiers seeking revenge. The KKK, South Carolina's Red Shirts, and Louisiana's Knights of the White Camellia were just a few of the secret societies

———————————— ✧ ————————————

This etching, made from a photograph of arrested Klansmen, shows how some of them disguised themselves.

that terrorized African Americans in the South. During Reconstruction, close to twenty thousand African Americans died, many lynched, hanged, or burned by angry whites.

SWING AROUND THE CIRCLE

That summer and fall, the president, General Grant, and several cabinet members toured the country in what Johnson called his "Swing Around the Circle" to build support for his views. The president still hoped to create a new party of Democrats and moderate Republicans. But Radical Republican hecklers booed Johnson. They yelled for the popular Grant and blamed the president for the murders of African Americans in the South. Johnson acted less than presidential. He cursed the unruly crowd.

The congressional elections of fall 1866 proved to be Johnson's downfall. Republicans swept most states. In Congress, Republicans outnumbered Democrats by well over the two-thirds majority needed to override any presidential veto. Johnson's hope for a third party was dashed. One observer noted, "He attempts to govern after he has lost the means to govern. He is like a general fighting without an army." Still Johnson refused to yield. In December 1866, he sent a message to Congress rejecting its version of Reconstruction. A congressman who tried to reason with the president said Johnson "got as ugly as the Devil. He was regularly mad . . . and couldn't talk like a reasonable being."

President Johnson looks to a portrait of George Washington for inspiration.

CHAPTER SEVEN

IMPEACHED!

Mr. Senator, how say you?
Is the respondent, Andrew Johnson,
President of the United States, guilty
or not guilty of the high misdemeanor, as
charged in this article?
—Senate clerk

The new year brought new trouble for President Johnson. By early spring 1867, Congress was flexing its muscle, showing the president how little power he had. On March 2, 1867, Congress began Reconstruction programs in the South. The president, increasingly isolated, could only watch from the White House.

Radical Reconstruction was under way. Congress divided the South into five military districts, each governed by a former Union general. Federal troops were stationed throughout the South to make sure all male citizens were allowed to vote. Southerners called it "bayonet rule."

Also in March 1867, Congress showed its disrespect for the White House by passing the Tenure of Office Act. The law forbade the president from firing any cabinet officer without notifying Congress. It was an attempt to force Johnson to keep Lincoln's appointed cabinet rather than naming Democrats who might have supported the beleaguered president. Every cabinet member opposed the Tenure Act, but Congress passed it anyway.

On August 12, 1867, President Johnson suspended Secretary of War Edwin Stanton. Johnson claimed, "It is impossible to get along with such a man in such a position and I can stand it no longer." Lincoln had appointed Stanton, who did not respect the new president and tried to undercut his policies. The president named Civil War hero Ulysses S. Grant as acting secretary. The Tenure of

Office Act required a president to notify Congress in writing about the dismissal of any cabinet officer. But since Congress was not in session during the summer, Johnson believed he was free to fire Stanton without telling Congress.

✧ ————————————

Edwin Stanton had a distinctive beard. He is easy to spot in many published drawings from Lincoln's and Johnson's presidencies.

Frozen Treasure

In 1867, while Johnson scuffled with Congress, his secretary of state, William Seward, completed a momentous land deal of about 586,400 square miles. The United States bought Alaska from the Russians for just over seven million dollars. Most newspapers and citizens mocked the real estate purchase, calling it "Andy's Ice Box" or "Seward's Folly." But the deal was profitable after gold, oil, and other valuable resources were discovered in the frozen land. Johnson's "Polar Bear Garden," with all its buried wealth, cost the United States just two cents an acre. The Alaska purchase greatly increased the size of the United States—and its strength. The man who had grown up in a poor, landless family understood the power of owning property. In another case, he vetoed giving government land to a New York mining company for too little money, saying, "The public domain is a national trust . . . not to be bestowed as a special privilege upon a favored class."

PREPARING FOR THE HEATED TERM.

King Andy and his man Billy lay in a great stock of Russian ice in order to cool down the Congressional majority.

────────── ✧

This cartoon humorously portrays Russian America (Alaska) as an iceberg in a wheelbarrow. It suggests that one good reason to buy it from Russia is to cool off Congress, who hotly oppose Johnson.

As General of the Army of the United States, Grant had a higher military rank than any American since George Washington. The Union general was wildly popular in the North. Johnson knew he had to please this powerful person, so it made sense to give him Stanton's job. But Grant didn't want to get stuck in the president's political battles. He reluctantly agreed to act as war secretary.

By December 1867, Congress was so unhappy with Johnson that the House of Representatives drafted a bill to impeach him. They were not able to pass the bill. Still Johnson was far from safe. In January 1868, the Senate voted to reinstate Stanton as secretary of war. Grant wanted no part of the political war. He stepped aside, and Stanton returned to his post. Meanwhile, the president ordered Grant, as commander of the army, to disregard orders from Stanton. The highest levels of the government were caught in a serious standoff. The president was not on speaking terms with his war secretary and did not want his top military commander to take orders from that war secretary.

Behind the scenes, Grant and fellow general William Sherman tried to persuade their boss, Secretary of War Stanton, to quit the War Department to ease tensions. He refused. Stanton's supporters included Radical Republican senator Charles Sumner, who sent Stanton a one-word telegram: "STICK."

By February 1868, the president was convinced that he and Stanton could not remain in the same administration. Johnson decided he needed to challenge the Tenure of Office Act and get rid of the stubborn war secretary. On February 21, 1868, Johnson dismissed Stanton and appointed Union general Lorenzo Thomas. But Stanton dug his heels in, literally locking himself in his office and refusing to leave. The next day, Stanton ordered the arrest of Thomas for seizing his office. Thomas posted a five-thousand-dollar bond to get out of jail and promptly returned to the War Department. He told Stanton, "The next time you have me arrested, please don't do it before I get something to eat." Stanton and Thomas had a whiskey together. Johnson was content to let the courts decide the matter. But Stanton dropped his charges, and soon Congress picked up the action.

At five o'clock on February 24, 1868, the House of Representatives voted 126 to 47 to impeach Andrew Johnson on charges he violated the Tenure of Office Act and other "high crimes and misdemeanors in office." It was the first time a U.S. president faced impeachment. House members called the president "a disgrace to this great and glorious age" and "the great criminal of our . . . country."

HOW IMPEACHMENT WORKS

Impeachment means to charge a president or other top government official with wrongdoing. The Constitution describes how the process works. Only the House of Representatives can vote to impeach a president. At the Senate trial that follows, the chief justice of the Supreme Court acts as the judge, and the Senate acts as the jury. If two-thirds of the senators find the president guilty of impeachment charges, he is convicted and is legally no longer president. Only two presidents have been impeached: Andrew Johnson and Bill Clinton. Neither man was convicted.

*Thaddeus Stevens delivers the last speech on impeachment
before the House votes to try Johnson in the Senate.*

———————————— ✧ ————————————

Johnson blamed Congress for his problems. He said,
"Haven't I been struggling ever since I have been in this chair
to uphold the Constitution they trample under foot?"

The president was very unpopular, but his accusers also
received their share of scorn. Three of the congressmen leading the impeachment drive—Representatives Thaddeus
Stevens and Benjamin Butler and Senator Benjamin Franklin
Wade—were linked to a financial scheme to pay off some
national bonds with greenbacks, or paper dollars, which
were not guaranteed to keep their value as well as gold. The
country's economy was tied to gold, considered to be the most
reliable financial base. Business leaders hated the greenback

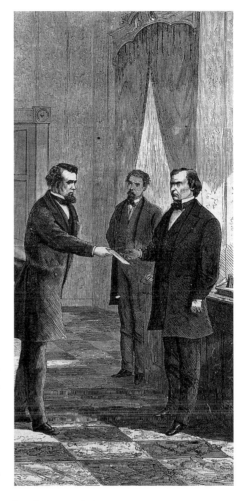

George T. Brown (left), the Senate's sergeant at arms (messenger), formally notifies Johnson (far right) of the upcoming Senate impeachment trial.

——————————— ✧

plan. Conservative Thomas W. Egan wrote Johnson, "All the great Northern Capitalists are afraid of the consequences of impeachment. To use the words of one of them—'The President might be crushed, but the finances of the country would go to ruin.'"

As president Johnson had never appointed a vice president. If Johnson were convicted, the president pro tempore (the Senate's presiding officer)—Benjamin Franklin Wade—would become the country's president. Johnson's supporters claimed Wade intended to share presidential power with Thaddeus Stevens and Ulysses Grant. Some citizens questioned whether Wade had a conflict of interest in voting on any impeachment matters.

The impeachment trial began on March 13, 1868. A board of managers—composed of seven members of the House of Representatives—presented the case against President Johnson. Five of the managers were Radical Republicans: Thaddeus Stevens, Benjamin Butler, George Boutwell, John Logan, and Thomas Williams. The remaining two House managers, John Bingham and James Wilson, were moderates.

The president selected both Democrats and Republicans to represent him at the trial. Johnson's team included Attorney General Henry Stanbery, who resigned from the cabinet to avoid a conflict of interest. Johnson's lawyers forbade him from giving interviews. They believed the blunt Southerner's off-the-cuff comments could only help his enemies.

The Senate impeachment trial of Andrew Johnson lasted sixty-five days.

A section of the Senate gallery (balcony) was reserved for women during Johnson's trial (top). Newspaper reporters worked hard to gather daily news of the trial (bottom).

─────────── ✧ ───────────

The public was riveted to the impeachment proceedings. People stood in line for hours to get a free ticket to watch the trial. Salmon P. Chase, chief justice of the Supreme Court, who also hoped to become president someday, oversaw the proceedings. According to rumors, Chase didn't want his rival, Senator Wade, to become president. Supposedly, the chief justice urged senators to vote not guilty.

Johnson never attended the trial, choosing to remain in the White House. But his servant, Warden, sat in on the trail daily. When he returned to the White House, the president would cheerfully ask him, "Well, Warden, what are the signs of the Zodiac today?"

Salmon P. Chase

——————— ◇ ———————

In closing arguments, manager George Boutwell told senators that if they acquitted Johnson, "You surrender the government into the hands of an . . . unscrupulous [immoral] man." Johnson's lawyer, Thomas Nelson, countered, "It almost shocks me to think that the President of the United States is to be dragged out of his office by these miserable little questions."

HOPE AND FEAR IN EVERY FACE

The Senate vote to decide Andrew Johnson's fate came on May 16. The Radical Republicans could count on thirty-five votes. They needed only one more vote to oust the president. Only one senator still remained undecided—Edmund G. Ross of Kansas.

The night before the vote, Ross received a telegram: "Kansas has heard the evidence and demands the conviction of the President. (Signed) D. R. Anthony and 1,000 others." Ross later recounted the historic scene in the packed Senate chamber: "Every individual in that great audience seemed distinctly visible. . . . Every fan was folded, not a foot moved, not the rustle of a garment, not a whisper was heard. . . . Hope and fear seemed blended in every face." Ross knew his vote would determine the political future of at least two men: Andrew Johnson and himself. "I almost literally looked down into my open grave," Ross would say later.

——————— ✧

The result of Johnson's impeachment trial hinged on one man's vote, Senator Edmond G. Ross.

YEAS.		NAYS.
1 Guilty	Anthony	
	Bayard	Not guilty 1
	Buckalew	Not guilty 2
2 Guilty	Cameron	
3 Guilty	Cattell	
Guilty	Chandler	
Guilty	Cole	
Guilty	Conkling	
Guilty	Conness	
Guilty	Corbett	
Guilty	Cragin	
	Davis	Not guilty 3
	Dixon	Not guilty 4
	Doolittle	Not guilty 5
Guilty	Drake	
Guilty	Edmunds	
Guilty	Ferry	
	Fessenden	Not guilty 6
	Fowler	Not guilty 7
Guilty	Frelinghuysen	
	Grimes	Not guilty 8
Guilty	Harlan	
	Henderson	Not guilty 9
	Hendricks	Not guilty 10
Guilty	Howard	
Guilty	Howe	
	Johnson	Not guilty 11
	McCreery	Not guilty 12
Guilty	Morgan	
Guilty	Morrill, of Maine	
Guilty	Morrill, of Vt.	
Guilty	Morton	
	Norton	Not guilty 13
Guilty	Nye	
Guilty	Patterson, of N. H.	
	Patterson, of Tenn.	Not guilty 14
Guilty	Pomeroy	
Guilty	Ramsey	
	Ross	Not guilty 15
	Saulsbury	Not guilty 16
Guilty	Sherman	
Guilty	Sprague	
Guilty	Stewart	
Guilty	Sumner	
Guilty	Thayer	
Guilty	Tipton	
	Trumbull	Not guilty 17
	Van Winkle	Not guilty 18
	Vickers	Not guilty 19
Guilty	Wade	
Guilty	Willey	
Guilty	Williams	
Guilty	Wilson	
Guilty	Yates	

35   19

MAY 11, 1868.

The Senate clerk asked each member, "Mr. Senator, how say you? Is the respondent, Andrew Johnson, President of the United States, guilty or not guilty of the high misdemeanor, as charged in this article?" The thirty-five senators voted guilty, as expected. Before the hushed crowd, Senator Ross answered, "Not guilty." By a vote of thirty-five to nineteen, Andrew Johnson had been impeached, but he had avoided conviction. The outcome was just that one vote short of the two-thirds needed to convict him.

The president's bodyguard, Colonel William Crook, raced back to 1600 Pennsylvania Avenue to report the vote. The president was in the White House library with friends, and he heard the news first via telegraph. Tears coursed down Johnson's face when he learned he was acquitted.

✧ ————————

Senators' votes for or against convicting Johnson were recorded by hand.

Crook ran upstairs to tell Eliza. The First Lady was sitting in a rocking chair, sewing. "He's acquitted! The president is acquitted," Crook exclaimed. "Crook," Eliza answered, "I knew he would be acquitted; I knew it."

Johnson announced, "It is a victory not for myself but for the Constitution and the country." His attorneys raced to the White House, which was opened to crowds of well-wishers. House manager Thaddeus Stevens heard the verdict and yelled, "The country is going to the devil."

Wooden markers (above) were painful reminders of the thousands of lives lost in the Civil War. The first Decoration Day, May 30, 1868, was organized by a veteran's organization to put flowers on dead soldiers' graves. It later became known as Memorial Day.

CHAPTER EIGHT

LIFE AFTER IMPEACHMENT

*I don't know anything more depressing than for
a man to labor for the people and not be
understood. It is enough to sour his soul.*
—Andrew Johnson

Two weeks after Johnson was acquitted, the North once
again turned its attention to the war dead. May 30, 1868,
had been declared Decoration Day, a time to place flowers
on the graves of Union soldiers. (The South had three different dates to remember their soldiers.) Later, Decoration
Day evolved into Memorial Day, a time to honor all those
who died, especially those who died for their country.

Andrew Johnson still had almost a year left to serve as
president. He hoped the Democrats would nominate him
to another term. They didn't, and he was bitterly disappointed. Still, he did his best to continue leading the
nation. On the Fourth of July, he granted a general
amnesty, or pardon, to all Confederates, except those who

had been accused of crimes. Three days later, Representative Thaddeus Stevens, who was near death and had to be carried up the steps of the Capitol to the House of Representatives, again attempted to have Johnson impeached. Few others had the stomach for more impeachment. Stevens died on August 11, 1868. Only Lincoln's funeral had drawn more mourners. The Radical Republican chose to be buried in a cemetery that contained the remains of people both black and white.

The country was slowly trying to mend the deep divisions caused by four years of bloodshed. One prominent North Carolinian said, "Through Andrew Johnson, and such as he, we begin to see how it is possible to love our whole country once more."

On November 3, 1868, Ulysses S. Grant was elected president. A month later, President Johnson sent Congress his last State of the Union message. Once again, Johnson focused on the rights of whites, saying, "The attempt to place the white population under the domination of persons of color in the South . . . has prevented the cooperation between the two races so essential to the success of the industrial enterprise [the U.S. economy]."

On Christmas Day 1868, President Johnson granted a final pardon to all Confederates, including Confederate president Jefferson Davis. Some Northerners were outraged that the president was willing to forgive the defeated South.

Four days later, on December 29, 1868, Johnson celebrated his sixtieth birthday with hundreds of friends, relatives, and supporters. The president's grandchildren and their dance school classmates entertained officials by demonstrating the waltz, promenade, and other dances.

Johnson's sixtieth birthday party was his last White House party.

Ulysses Grant didn't allow his children to attend what he called the "Juvenile Soiree." The war, politics, and impeachment had left in him deep feelings of anger and distrust.

The day before the new president's inauguration, Ulysses Grant told officials he would not ride in a carriage with outgoing President Johnson. The two men did not speak to one another. Johnson's bitterness showed on his last day in office. On March 4, 1869, while most of Washington prepared to watch General Grant take the oath of office, Johnson chose to boycott the inauguration. He remained at his desk in the White House, with his cabinet members, whom he forbade to attend Grant's swearing-in. "I think we will finish our work here without going to the Capitol," Johnson told the cabinet. Eliza and the rest of the Johnson family had already left the mansion. At noon, when his presidency was officially over, Johnson quietly said good-bye to the White House staff, climbed into a carriage, and left. He had come to Washington four years earlier as Lincoln's vice president. He had been thrust into power, then almost pushed out of office. It was time to go home to Tennessee.

"WELCOME HOME, ANDY"

Some fifteen thousand supporters lined up to welcome the Johnsons back to Greeneville. In 1861, when Johnson had fled his home during the Civil War to go to Washington, Greeneville had hung a huge "Andy Johnson, traitor" banner across Main Street. Times had changed. The new sign stretched across Main Street read, "Welcome Home, Andrew Johnson, Patriot."

The former president quoted Cardinal Thomas Wolsey, an English statesman who had been charged with treason three hundred years earlier:

> *An old man broken with the storms of state*
> *Is come to lay his weary bones among ye,*
> *Give him a little earth for charity.*

The Johnsons began repairing their home, which had been used as a military hospital during the war. Years of neglect had worn down the property. A *New York Herald* reporter wrote, "The fences of the lot and windows of the house show evident signs of dilapidation." Adjusting to life in a small town after living in the White House wasn't easy. Johnson went on a speaking tour. Thousands of people turned out to hear him attack President Grant, claiming, "He hasn't a single idea. He has no policy, no conception of what the country requires . . . . He is mendacious [dishonest], cunning, and treacherous." When the tour ended, Johnson returned to Greeneville, which, he wrote to his youngest son, Frank, was "a dull place and likely to continue so."

The former president decided to run for Congress. Johnson said, "I would rather have the vindication [freedom from blame] of my state by electing me to my old seat in the Senate of the United States than to be monarch of the grandest empire on earth." Son Robert committed suicide after years of alcoholism. Eliza remained in poor health. Johnson was desperate for some role in politics again. He wrote his daughter Martha, "I long to be set free from this place forever I hope." He ran unsuccessfully in both 1869 and 1872.

✧

In this modern reconstruction of Johnson's bedroom in his Greeneville home, his hat rests on the bureau (left). Compared to Washington, D.C., Greeneville seemed dull to the former president.

In 1873 a deadly outbreak of cholera hit Greeneville and killed one hundred people. Although other wealthy families fled town, the Johnsons stayed to help care for their sick neighbors. Johnson became sick and never fully recovered.

VICTORY, APPLAUSE, AND FLOWERS

At last, Johnson had his wish. The Tennessee legislature was deeply divided, but after fifty-five ballots, they finally voted to send Andrew Johnson back to Washington as a senator.

On March 5, 1875, Johnson returned to the Senate. He is the only president who became a senator after serving in the White House. (President John Quincy Adams served in the House of Representatives for eighteen years after leaving the White House.) Johnson's fellow senators stood to applaud the sixty-six-year-old leader. Camellias covered his desk, leaving him blushing and teary-eyed. Grant's vice president, Henry Wilson, who had voted to convict President Johnson at the impeachment trial, called the Senate to order. Senator Johnson had told supporters that he would not dwell on the past. "I will go to the Senate, with no personal hostility toward any one . . . . My few remaining years shall be devoted to the weal [well-being] and prosperity of my country which I love more than my own life." The *New York Nation* noted, "His personal integrity is beyond questions and his respect for the laws and the Constitution made his administration a remarkable contrast to that which succeeded it."

Johnson claimed he held no animosity toward anyone, but during his years in exile in Greeneville, he often attacked President Grant in his talks. On March 22, 1875, the new senator stood to make what would be his only speech from the Senate. He spoke for three hours, criticizing Grant's administration. Two days later, Congress adjourned and Johnson returned home once again.

On July 27, 1875, Andrew Johnson was visiting his daughter Mary. After lunch he went upstairs to rest. He fell down, his left side paralyzed by a stroke. Johnson told his family not to call the doctor. Instead, his wife and children gathered by his side. Although his speech was slurred, he spoke of his childhood, recounting important events in his life. Three days later, Andrew Johnson suffered a second stroke. He died on July 31, 1875.

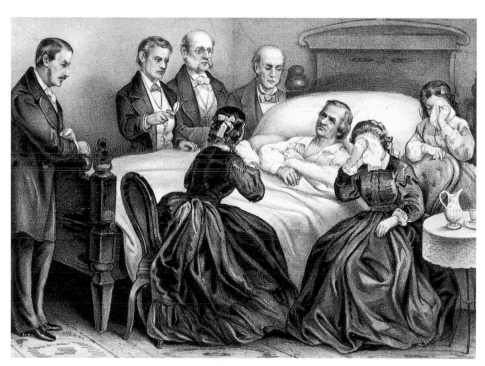

As Andrew Johnson lay dying, his wife and family gathered around his bed.

Dignitaries begin to gather (lower right) for Johnson's funeral.
The funeral procession included five thousand people.

Years earlier, President Johnson had told students at Yale University that the only regret he had about his life was failing to choose the right profession. Andrew Johnson, the man who never attended school in his life, said he wished he had been a schoolmaster. The child of poor illiterates who didn't learn to read until he was a teenager would die the richest man in town. His estate was valued at one hundred thousand dollars. But Johnson's goal in life was not money. He cared, instead, about doing what he thought was right.

Andrew Johnson believed he had always been loyal to his country and to the Constitution. He told his family, "When I die, I desire no better winding sheet [covering for a dead body] than the Stars and Stripes, and no softer pillow than the Constitution of my country." Andrew Johnson's body, wrapped in the flag and cushioned by the Constitution, is buried overlooking his hometown of Greeneville.

Although Andrew Johnson's faith in Americans may have held firm, the country's memories of the seventeenth president have shifted. The uneducated tailor worked hard and ended up in the White House, but many consider him one of the country's least successful presidents. In a way, Andy Johnson never grew beyond his childhood ideas about what poor whites deserved—and blacks didn't.

———————————— ◆

A statue of an eagle guards Johnson's grave. The monument is engraved with the epitaph, "His faith in the people never wavered."

TIMELINE

1808   Andrew Johnson is born in Raleigh, North Carolina.

1827   Johnson marries Eliza McCardle in Greeneville, Tennessee.

1828   Johnson wins his first election as Greeneville's alderman. Daughter Martha is born.

1830   Son Charles is born.

1832   Daughter Mary is born.

1834   Son Robert is born. Johnson is elected Greeneville's mayor, then state legislator.

1842   Johnson is elected U.S. representative from Tennessee.

1852   Son Andrew Jr. (known as Frank) is born.

1853   Johnson is elected governor of Tennessee.

1857   Johnson is appointed U.S. senator. He is injured in a train derailment on the way to Washington, D.C.

1860   Abraham Lincoln is elected president. South Carolina secedes from the Union.

1861   Civil War begins when Confederates fire on Fort Sumter.

1862   President Lincoln names Johnson military governor of Tennessee.

1863   Son Charles dies.

1864   Johnson is elected vice president.

1865   Confederate general Robert E. Lee surrenders to Union general Ulysses S. Grant. President Lincoln is shot at Ford's Theatre. Lincoln dies, and Johnson is sworn in as president. Johnson grants amnesty to most Confederates. The Thirteenth Amendment becomes law.

1866 Johnson vetoes the Freedmen's Bureau Bill, but Congress overrides the veto. Johnson vetoes the Civil Rights Act. Congress overrides the Civil Rights veto. Johnson begins the "Swing Around the Circle" election tour.

1867 Johnson vetoes the Tenure of Office Act and the first Reconstruction Act on the same day. Congress overrides both vetoes. The Senate approves the United States' purchase of Alaska from Russia.

1868 Johnson fires Secretary of War Edwin Stanton. The House votes 126 to 47 to impeach Johnson. The Senate acquits Johnson. The Fourteenth Amendment becomes law. Ulysses S. Grant is elected president. Johnson grants final pardon to all Confederates.

1869 Johnson and his family leave Washington, D.C., and return to Greeneville, Tennessee. Son Robert dies.

1875 Johnson is returned to the U.S. Senate. Johnson dies at daughter Mary's home in Carter's Station, Tennessee.

SOURCE NOTES

7   Hans L. Trefousse, *Andrew Johnson: A Biography* (New York: W. W. Norton and Company, 1989), 242.
8   Zachary Kent, *Encyclopedia of Presidents: Andrew Johnson* (Chicago: Children's Press, 1989), 12.
8   Ibid., 13.
9   Cathy East Dubowski, *Andrew Johnson: Rebuilding the Union* (Englewood Cliffs, NJ: Silver Burdett Press, 1991), 49.
10 Wilmer L. Jones, PhD., *After the Thunder: Fourteen Men Who Shaped Post-Civil War America* (Dallas: Taylor Publishing Company, 2000), 111.
12 Trefousse, 23.
13 Dubowski, 21.
13 Kent, 17.
14 Trefousse, 23
16 Dubowski, 25.
16 Trefousse, 27.
16 Kent, 19.
17 Dubowski, 30.
19 Ibid., 32.
19 Kent, 22.
19–20   Ibid.
21 Ibid.
22 Ibid., 24.
22 Jones, 113.
23 Trefousse, 44.
24 Alan Brinkley and Davis Dyer, eds., *The Reader's Companion to the American Presidency* (New York: Houghton Mifflin Co., 2000), 203.
24 Trefousse, 45.
25 Brinkley and Dyer, 204.
26 Kent, 27.
26 Trefousse, 73.
27–28   Dubowski, 40.
28 Ibid., 41.

29 Kent, 29.
29 Dubowski, 43.
31 Kent, 12.
31–32   Dubowski, 43.
32 Kent, 7.
32 Trefousse, 131.
33 Ibid.
33 Ibid.
34 Kent, 37.
35 Brinkley and Dyer, 205.
35 Kent, 37.
36 Ibid., 39.
37 Trefousse, 156.
37 Kent, 39.
38 Geoffrey C. Ward, *The Civil War: An Illustrated History* (New York: Alfred A. Knopf, 1990), 166.
39 Ibid., 95.
40 Trefousse, 168.
40 Ibid., 168.
41 Ibid., 183.
43 Ibid., 191.
43 Ward, 360.
44 Trefousse, 191.
44 Jones, 115.
44–45   Carter Smith, ed., *One Nation Again: A Sourcebook on the Civil War* (Brookfield, CT: The Millbrook Press, 1993), 44.
47 Trefousse, 194.
47 Jones, 115.
48 Trefousse, 239.
48 Carl Sferrazza Anthony, *America's First Families: An Inside View of 200 Years of Private Life in the White House* (New York: Simon and Schuster, 2000), 308.
50 Brooks D. Simpson, *The Reconstruction Presidents* (Lawrence: The University Press of Kansas, 1998), 67.
51 Ibid., 67.
51 Trefousse, 196.
52 Brinkley and Dyer, 205.

52 Ibid., 204.
54 Brendan January,
    Cornerstones of Freedom:
    Reconstruction (Danbury, CT:
    Children's Press, 1999), 11.
54 Trefousse, 191.
58–59 Brinkley and Dyer, 206.
59 Simpson, 76.
59 Ibid., 86.
60 Ibid., 76.
60 Ibid., 78.
60 January, 13.
61 Joy Hakim, *A History of US:*
    Reconstruction and Reform,
    2nd ed. (New York: Oxford
    University Press, 1999), 21.
62 Anthony, 105.
64 Dubowski, 7.
64 Kent, 61.
64–65 Simpson, 87.
66 Trefousse, 253.
67 Simpson, 98.
67 Ibid.
67 Trefousse, 243.
68 January, 9.
68 Smith, 50.
68 Ibid., 52.
69 Ibid., 50.
71 Trefousse, 244.
72 Smith, 58.
72 Brinkley and Dyer, 208.
72 January, 15.
72 Trefousse, 247.
74 Ibid., 267.
74–75 Ibid., 284.
75 Ibid., 260.
75 Ibid., 253.
76 Ibid, 242.
77 January, 24.
77 Ibid.
79 Trefousse, 271.
81 Dubowski, 107.
81 Smith, 64.
82 Kent, 71.
83 Trefousse, 260.
84 Ibid., 313.
85 Ibid., 314.
85 Kent, 73.
86 Dubowski, 106.
87 Trefousse, 302.
90 Kent, 75.

90 Ibid., 76.
90 Ibid.
91 Ibid., 77.
91 Ibid., 78.
91 Ibid.
92 Dubowski, 107.
93 Ibid., 108.
93 Kent, 81.
93 Trefousse, 327.
95 Dubowski, 117.
96 Kent, 81.
96 Jones, 122.
97. Dubowski, 112.
98 Ibid., 113.
98 Kent, 86.
98–99 Trefousse, 356.
99 Ibid., 358.
99 Kent, 86.
99 Trefousse, 360.
100 Dubowski, 114.
100 Ibid.
103 Ibid., 115.
103 Juddi Morris, *At Home with*
    the Presidents (New York:
    John Wiley and Sons, 1999),
    69.

BIBLIOGRAPHY

Anthony, Carl Sferrazza. *America's First Families: An Inside View of 200 Years of Private Life in the White House.* New York: Simon and Schuster, 2000.

Brinkley, Alan, and Davis Dyer, eds. *The Reader's Companion to the American Presidency.* New York: Houghton Mifflin Co., 2000.

Catton, Bruce. *U.S. Grant and the American Military Tradition.* New York: Grosset & Dunlap, 1954.

Dubowski, Cathy East. *Andrew Johnson: Rebuilding the Union.* Englewood Cliffs, NJ: Silver Burdett Press, 1991.

Golay, Michael. *A Ruined Land: The End of the Civil War.* New York: John Wiley & Sons, 1999.

Hakim, Joy. *A History of US: Reconstruction and Reform.* 2nd ed. New York: Oxford University Press, 1999.

January, Brendan. *Cornerstones of Freedom: Reconstruction.* Danbury, CT: Children's Press, 1999.

Jones, Wilmer L., PhD. *After the Thunder: Fourteen Men Who Shaped Post-Civil War America.* Dallas: Taylor Publishing Company, 2000.

Kent, Zachary. *Encyclopedia of Presidents: Andrew Johnson.* Chicago: Children's Press, 1989.

McGinnis, Ralph Y., ed. *Quotations from Abraham Lincoln.* Chicago: Nelson-Hall, 1977.

Morris, Juddi. *At Home with the Presidents.* New York: John Wiley and Sons, 1999.

Rehnquist, William H. *Grand Inquests: The Historic Impeachments of Justice Samuel Chase and President Andrew Johnson.* New York: William Morrow and Company, 1992.

Simpson, Brooks D. *The Reconstruction Presidents.* Lawrence: The University Press of Kansas, 1998.

Smith, Carter, ed. *One Nation Again: A Sourcebook on the Civil War.* Brookfield, CT: The Millbrook Press, 1993.

Taylor, Tim. *The Book of Presidents.* New York: Arno Press, 1972.

Trefousse, Hans L. *Andrew Johnson: A Biography.* New York: W. W. Norton and Company, 1989.

Ward, Geoffrey C. *The Civil War: An Illustrated History.* New York: Alfred A. Knopf, 1990.

FURTHER READING AND WEBSITES

American Presidents: *Life Portraits*
<http://www.americanpresidents.org/presidents/president.asp?PresidentNumber=17>
This site offers a brief biography, photographs, and teaching guide for Johnson and other presidents in conjunction with the C-SPAN television series "American Presidents: Life Portraits."

Andrew Johnson National Historic Site
<http://www.nps.gov/anjo>
This site gives information about two Johnson family homes and Johnson's second tailor shop in Greeneville, Tennessee, managed as one national historic site.

Arnold, James R. *The Civil War.* Minneapolis: Lerner Publications Company, 2005.

Greene, Meg. *Into the Land of Freedom. African Americans in Reconstruction.* Minneapolis: Lerner Publications Company, 2004.

St. George, Judith, and David Small. *So You Want to Be President?* New York: Philomel, 2000.

The White House—Presidents—Andrew Johnson
<http://www.whitehouse.gov/history/presidents/aj17.html>
Read biographies of Johnson and his wife along with other presidents at this White House website.

INDEX

abolitionists, 35, 51, 60
Alaska purchase, 84
Andrew Johnson National Historic Site, 26

Black Codes, 60, 64, 72
board of managers, 88, 90; members: Boutwell, 88, 90; Butler, 86, 88; Logan, 88; Stevens, 73, 86, 87, 88, 93, 96; Williams, 88
Booth, John Wilkes, 51, 52
Brownlow, Parson William G., 22–23, 33, 66, 76

Civil Rights Act, 72, 74
Civil War, 7, 33, 73, 82, 98; beginning, 34, 38; casualties, 51, 56, 68; causes, 32, 34; effect on Americans, 63; Fort Sumter, 34, 38; in Tennessee (Shiloh), 38–39
Confederate army, 34, 37, 38, 40; generals in: Lee, 45, 46, 53
Confederate States of America (Confederacy), 7; capital, 44, 56; former leaders in Congress, 58; president, 8, 35, 53, 96

Davis, Jefferson, 8–9, 35, 53, 96. *See also* Confederate States of America (Confederacy)
Decoration Day, 94, 95
Doughty, Turner (stepfather), 16, 26
Douglass, Frederick, 77

Emancipation Proclamation, 40–41

Freedmen's Bureau, 67, 68–70, 71, 74

gerrymandering, 27–28
Grant, Ulysses S., 38, 39, 45, 46, 53, 79, 82, 84, 87, 96–97, 98, 100, 101

Greeneville, Tennessee, 8, 16, 19, 21, 36, 98, 99, 100, 102, 103

Homestead Bill, 25–26, 27, 32, 40

impeachment, 74, 84–93, 97

Johnson, Andrew: Andrew Johnson National Historic Site, 26; apprenticeship, 12–16; birth and childhood, 10–12; children, 20, 21, 22, 23, 24, 26, 36, 40, 41, 48, 62, 63, 99, 101; as congressman, 23–28; death, 101; education, 11, 13, 17, 20, 23, 102; election of 1864, 9, 41; as governor of Tennessee (elected), 28–29, 31; grandchildren, 48, 62; impeachment, 74, 84, 85–87, 97; impeachment trial, 88–93, 100; introduction to politics, 20; marriage, 16–17; as military governor of Tennessee, 9, 36–37; plot to kill, 51; post-presidency, 98–101; as president, 9, 17, 47–98, 102; as public servant, 20, 21–22; as senator, 7–9, 31–36, 100–101; siblings, 10, 12, 13; as tailor, 14, 16, 17, 18, 19–20, 21, 24, 28, 103; Tennessee Militia, 21, 23; as vice president, 43–47
Johnson, Andrew "Frank" Jr. (son), 26, 36, 48, 99
Johnson, Charles (son), 20, 22, 23, 24, 26, 35–36, 40
Johnson, Elizabeth (sister), 10, 12
Johnson, Eliza McCartle (wife), 16, 17, 20, 22, 24, 26, 36, 40, 48, 61, 63, 93, 97, 99, 101
Johnson, Jacob (father), 10, 11, 12
Johnson, Martha (daughter), 20, 22, 23, 24, 26, 36, 48, 62, 63, 99
Johnson, Mary (daughter), 21, 22, 23,

24, 26, 36, 41, 48, 62, 63, 101
Johnson, Mary McDonough (mother),
    10, 11, 12, 13, 16, 26, 36
Johnson, Robert (son), 21, 22, 23, 24,
    26, 36, 40, 48, 63, 99
Johnson, William (brother), 10, 12,
    13, 14, 15, 16, 64

Ku Klux Klan. *See* secret societies

Land Act. *See* Homestead Bill
Lee, Robert E., 45, 46, 53
Lincoln, Abraham, 9, 32, 34, 35, 36,
    40, 42, 43, 44, 45, 46, 50, 52, 54,
    73, 75, 79, 82, 87, 96, 98; death,
    46–47; election of 1864, 41

National Woman Suffrage Association,
    72

Patterson, David Trotter (son-in-law),
    48

race riot: Memphis, 75, 76; New
    Orleans, 77
Radical Republicans, 50, 52, 60, 64,
    66, 71, 72, 73, 75, 79, 84, 88, 90,
    96; members: Boutwell, 88, 90;
    Butler, 86, 88; Chandler, 73; Logan,
    88, Stevens, 73, 86, 87, 88, 93, 96;
    Sumner, 73, 77, 84; Wade, 52, 73,
    86, 87, 89; Williams, 88
Reconstruction, 54–65, 79; Radical
    Reconstruction, 81
Ross, Edmund G., 90–91, 92

secret societies: Knights of the White
    Camellias, 78; Ku Klux Klan, 78;
    Red Shirts, 78
Selby, James, 12, 13, 14
slaves (slavery), 22, 24, 25, 31, 32, 33,
    35, 36, 40, 41, 55, 58, 60, 61, 63,
    65, 67, 68, 69; in Union army, 59,
    60, 75

Stanton, Edwin, 82, 84, 85
Stevens, Thaddeus, 73, 86, 87, 88, 93,
    96
Sumner, Charles, 73, 77, 84

Tenure of Office Act, 81–82, 84, 85

Union army, 36, 40, 41, 49, 56, 63;
    generals in: Grant, 38, 39, 45, 46,
    53, 79, 82, 84, 87, 96–97, 98, 100,
    101; Sherman, 39, 52–53, 69, 84;
    Thomas, 85; slaves in, 59, 60, 75
U.S. Congress, 8, 23, 26, 27, 28, 32,
    35, 58, 61, 64, 65, 66, 67, 68, 71,
    72, 73, 74, 75, 76, 79, 81, 82, 83,
    85, 86, 96, 99, 101. *See also* U.S.
    House of Representatives; U.S.
    Senate
U.S. Constitution, 7, 22, 36, 55, 59,
    85, 86, 93, 100, 103; Thirteenth
    Amendment, 61, 64–65; Fourteenth
    Amendment, 76, 77
U.S. House of Representatives, 27, 84,
    85, 88, 96, 100
U.S. Senate, 31, 32, 84, 85, 86, 88,
    89, 90, 99, 100, 101

Wade, Benjamin Franklin, 52, 73, 86,
    87, 89

ABOUT THE AUTHOR

Kate Havelin was in junior high when she decided to be a writer. She edited her high school and college newspapers and studied journalism. After graduating, she worked as a television producer for more than a decade. This is Havelin's eleventh book for young readers. She lives with her husband and two sons in St. Paul, Minnesota.

PHOTO ACKNOWLEDGMENTS

Photographs in this book appear with the permission of: Library of Congress, pp. 2 (LC-B8184-10690), 6 (LC-USZ61-181), 9 (Printed Ephemera Collection; Portfolio 137, Folder 22d), p. 21 (LC-USZ62-130976), 26 (LC-USZ62-113574), 27 (HABS-TENN-30-GRNV-19), 29 (LC-USZ62-503), 30 (LC-USZC4-4589), 33 (LC-USZ62-116284), 34 (LC-USZC4-528), 37 (LC-USZ62-35074), 39 (LC-USZ62-3581), 42 (LC-USZ62-2046), 44 (LC-USZ62-117574), 45 (LC-USZ62-2070), 46 (LC-USZ62-2074), 48 (LC-DIG-cwpbh-00194), 51 (LC-USZC4-6468), 53 (LC-USZ62-132504), 55 (LC-USZC4-9374), 56 (LC-USZ62-107050), 57 (LC-USZ62-15649), 59 (LC-USZ62-2048), 62 (LC-USZ62-25821), 69 (LC-USZ62-105555), 70 (LC-USZ62-121633), 73 (LC-DIG-cwpbh-00460), 74 (LC-USZ62-127597), 76 (LC-USZ62-111152), 77 (right) (LC-USZ62-126782), 78 (LC-USZ62-913442), 80 (LC-USZ62-11142), 82 (LC-DIG-cwpb-06437), 83 (LC-USZ62-61346), 86 (LC-USZ62-106848), 87 (LC-USZ62-106849), 88 (LC-USZ62-1732), 89 (top) (LC-USZ62-119581), 90 (LC-DIG-cwpbh-00518), 91 (LC-DIG-cwpbh-00557), 94 (LC-DIG-cwpb-00494), 99 (LC-G613-77387), 101 (LC-USZ62-2240), 102 (LC-USZ62-86250); Tennessee State Library and Archives, pp. 11, 18, 63, 67; Dover Publications, p. 12; Carlyle Campbell Library, Meredith College, Raleigh, NC, p. 15; The Special Collections Library of the University of Tennessee, Knoxville, Tennessee, pp. 23, 25, 47, 97; National Archives, pp. 38, 49, 92; Andrew Johnson National Historic Site, pp. 36, 103; General Research Division The New York Public Library, pp. 71, 89 (bottom); Dictionary of American Portraits, p. 77 (left).

Cover: Library of Congress (LC-USZ62-13017)